Praise for Gary Joseph Grappo:

Get the Job You Want in Thirty Days

"Don't interview without this book! It's loaded with simple, straightforward advice that can make all the difference in getting the job."
  —Gloria Rosen Koznesoff, John Hancock Financial Services

"From writing the resume to clinching the job, this book takes you step-by-step and tells you what to do to succeed."
  —Leon N. Graham, Executive Vice President, BMG Direct

"Essential information on resumes, interviews, networking, and more . . . This book is a gold mine for the job seeker!"
  —Carol Eicher, Director of Human Resources,
    The Lodge of Four Seasons

"A clear, concise, easy-to-use book no job seeker should be without."

  —Steven Leek, Director of Sales Training,
    Edison Menswear Group

The Top 10 Fears of Job Seekers

"An excellent resource for turning career stress into career success."

  —Scott DeGarmo, Editor-in-Chief and Publisher,
    Success magazine

"Gary Grappo goes beyond typical self-help cliches to offer truly valuable guidance for the job hunter."
  —Robert K. Prescott, Director, Corporate Services and Instructor in Business Administration, The Smeal College of Business at Pennsylvania State University

Berkley Books by Gary Joseph Grappo

GET THE JOB YOU WANT IN THIRTY DAYS

THE TOP 10 FEARS OF JOB SEEKERS

THE TOP 10 CAREER STRATEGIES FOR THE YEAR 2000 AND BEYOND

THE TOP 10 CAREER STRATEGIES FOR THE YEAR 2000 & BEYOND

Gary Joseph Grappo

B

BERKLEY BOOKS, NEW YORK

This book is an original publication of The Berkley Publishing Group.

THE TOP 10 CAREER STRATEGIES FOR THE YEAR 2000 & BEYOND

A Berkley Book / published by arrangement with
the author

PRINTING HISTORY
Berkley trade paperback edition / August 1997

The Putnam Berkley World Wide Web site address is
http://www.berkley.com

ISBN: 0-425-15792-X

BERKLEY®
Berkley Books are published by The Berkley Publishing Group,
200 Madison Avenue, New York, New York 10016.
BERKLEY and the "B" design
are trademarks belonging to Berkley Publishing Corporation.

PRINTED IN THE UNITED STATES OF AMERICA

10 9 8 7 6 5 4 3 2 1

For Jim and Paula Grappo,
excessive, compulsive workers
who raised one

Acknowledgments

As Charles Handy once said, "The future we predict today is not inevitable." Nevertheless, people like Charles Handy, Ken Blanchard, Tom Peters, Alvin Toffler, and numerous other writers listed in the bibliography of this book have, along with myself, attempted to offer intelligent insight into that which has not yet occurred. The process on some levels is scientific and on other levels is admittedly educated guesswork. In the latter, one is willing to go out on a limb in order to provide potentially valuable insights to others to improve their quality of life.

To the many writers and futurists who have helped inspire this book, I wish to say thank you from all of us for taking the time to think, dream, care, and share. Also, I wish to acknowledge the many individuals who attend my seminars around the United States and those who write me as well. Often I learn the most from you. You have contributed valuable insights into the shaping and publication of this work.

Writing this book has energized me and excited me about the future. It has made me less fearful and quite exhilarated about its possibilities. Upon completing this writing, I am extremely optimistic about what lies ahead for all of us. I hope reading it will help inspire you to believe and feel the same.

Contents

Contents

Contents

Contents

INTRODUCTION

Unsettling Changes Reshaping Our Lives and Work

Alvin Toffler, in his now-famous work *Future Shock*, considers *change* as the foremost issue facing the world today. In 1970, when the book was first published, he wrote, "In the three short decades between now and the twenty-first century, millions of ordinary, psychologically normal people will face an abrupt collision with the future. Citizens of the world's richest and most technologically advanced nations will find it increasingly painful to keep up with the incessant demand for change that characterizes our time. For them the future will have arrived too soon." Because you have selected this book to read, you have already ascertained that your world and the world of work have collided

1

with the future very much along the lines described in Toffler's prophetic words written decades ago.

Old Game, New Rules

We are increasingly living in an age where the "normal" way of doing things in our jobs and careers has virtually disappeared. It's the same game but with new rules. How would you feel if you were playing a game with friends, a card game perhaps, and they played by completely different rules? Has that type of situation ever happened to you? You probably felt frustrated and possibly even angry. Many, as their careers collide with the future, are experiencing the same frustration and anger with the career game in the new world of work.

For example, not many years ago, we commuted to work. Now, many are increasingly telecommuting. Expert opinion projects that millions of corporations will have formal telecommuting policies in place by the beginning of the next century. Consider that not long ago, job seekers attended job fairs to network and find a job. Now the catchwords are "meet me at the Internet CyberFair" where virtual job fairs have gone mainstream. Further, the abbreviations and acronyms of the past have been quickly replaced with techno lingo. We now live in a world of BBS, bps, RAM, Gopher, MB, WWW, and E-mail to mention a few. Yet many remain techno illiterate.

The new information-age employer is also driven by rapidly changing technology. The result is more efficient work by fewer and more educated workers. Corporations are providing fewer and fewer employment opportunities. Neil DeCarlo, a Miami-based business consultant, states, "Instead, they [businesses] will partner, hook up, outsource, and parcel off tasks and activities to an increasingly transient workforce." A job, in the way we once knew it, will not exist. It is rapidly becoming extinct.

"The modern world is on the verge of another huge leap in creativity and productivity, but the job is not going to be part of tomorrow's economic reality," says *Fortune* magazine in the September 19, 1994, issue. "There still is and will always be enormous amounts of work to do, but it is not going to be contained in the familiar envelopes we call jobs."

A recent study reported in *Personnel Journal* was conducted by the National Commission for Employment Policy, a government advisory panel. It found that employees with strong job stability—defined as those with only one or no job changes in a ten-year period—decreased from 67 percent in the 1970s to 52 percent in the 1980s. The percentage of employees with weak stability—those changing employers at least three times in a ten-year period—doubled to 24 percent during the 1980s. Trends for the '90s had not yet been compiled at this printing; however, early projections indicate percentages will exceed those of the 1980s.

Embrace Change to Survive and Thrive

As you can see, so much is happening so quickly that there is a danger of becoming preoccupied with change. It seems as though no one can agree—the economists, the politicians and CEOs—on how to manage it. However, from an an individual's career perspective, it can be stated that change is managed in one of two ways: fight or flight. If flight is chosen, the bad news is, there *is* nowhere to run. It is futile to run from the inevitable. Embrace change, and you have chosen to fight. Herein is the option that gives you the ability to survive and thrive in the future climate of change.

Charles Handy, the author of the best-selling book, *The Age of Unreason*, agrees that embracing change is a way to manage it. In his new book, *The Age of Paradox*, he states, "Organizations will become both smaller and bigger at the same time; they will be flatter, more flexible, and more dispersed; similarly our working lives will have to be flatter and more flexible. Life will be unreasonable in the sense that it won't go on as it used to; *we shall have to make things happen for us rather than wait for them to happen.*" Throughout the 1990s, too many people for too many years have been unsettled by the changes in our technological world of work. The winners and survivors are those who face the changes head-on. But how do you do it?

The Top Ten Career Strategies

This book is about how to turn stressful change into successful survival. You will discover how to take the rapid change in your job and career and mold, shape, bend, and essentially take control of it to meet your unique employment needs. This book is about ten strategies to manage change so as to be successful at making a living in the year 2000 and beyond.

Strategy 1: Update Your Attitude

Here, you discover how to realign your attitude so as to not let a negative attitude about change and the future become a stumbling block to the realization of your goals. You will learn how anxiety prevents us from achieving the very things that we desire. In essence, the thing or things that we fear and obsess about the most, we may actually bring upon ourselves. You will find out how to make sure, through an update of your attitude, that your fears and anxieties are overcome. A positive attitude about change will create a positive reality.

Strategy 2: Discover the Future Growth Industries

This section covers up-to-date information about the future growth industries. You will learn about the companies that currently represent these growth industries. Also, you will learn how to research and discover companies that are continuously emerging as growth leaders and being added to the list of companies on the cutting edge. This section will aid you in becoming, if you're not already, a futurist. With this knowledge and information, you will have the necessary insights to beat the competition and keep your career at its peak potential well into the twenty-first century.

Strategy 3: Develop the Right Skills

Ken Blanchard, author of the best-seller *The One Minute Manager*, explained at a recent *Success* magazine conference that soft skills such as teamwork will be needed to survive in the leaner and flatter organizations of the twenty-first century. Besides the soft skills, you will also discover in this chapter the necessary hard skills that will be expected of the future worker. The hard skills are the ones relating to the new technology and information revolution that have dramatically redefined our work environment. You will want to read this section carefully and assess your own personal skills' strengths and weaknesses. Be prepared to make necessary improvements and changes to remain marketable and a leader in the future world of work.

Strategy 4: Learn to Sell Yourself Like a Company Sells a Product

Here you receive an overview of the practical self-selling skills needed to be a sales pro in the future competitive environment of companies that function with fewer employees, which will increase the number of layoffs and create enormous competition for the jobs that are available. You will want to understand and implement the sales techniques that are needed to be consistently employed in any market. Unique to this book, you learn how to create and use a *sight-seller*, or personal portfolio, to establish your credibility and sell yourself effectively.

Strategy 5: Build a Network

This chapter deals with the important but often misunderstood and overlooked issue of building a personal network of contacts. It covers why we network and how to do it. It explains how to make networking a lifestyle and not just an exercise to get you out of a jam when you're unemployed. You learn how to have a ready-made arsenal of contacts that you can call upon whenever you need them, no matter what unfortunate turn in your career may come your way. This chapter will review a broad base of networking actions that you will want to integrate into your daily lifestyle. Even if you think you have no need for a job at the current time, this chapter reinforces your ongoing need for contacts. In a time when downsizing is often sudden and unexpected, this section is critical to understand and implement.

Strategy 6: Change Jobs Frequently

The new business environment demands that we do not sit idle and settle into a comfort zone with our jobs. It is the kind of world that you can't get too comfortable in. The only individuals suited for survival are those who are adventurous. Gone are the days of basking in the same position for years and years. You will constantly have to be taking action and moving on to the next frontier.

Strategy six covers the idea of the fear of change that is common among most workers today. It reveals how to position yourself for an internal change and promote up in the company for which you are currently working. It also gives you the tools to make an external change to another company while you are still employed. You learn the telltale signs of a comfort zone that could be hindering your career. It may actually set you up for an unhealthy, codependent relationship with an employer and expose you to the risk of a major career setback. You discover the importance of a *forced* job change at various intervals in your career whether you feel like you are ready for it or not—whether you feel like there is a need for it or not.

Strategy 7: Act as an Independent Contractor

This section covers the importance of acquiring the attitude of an independent contractor in order to thrive in the new job market.

You discover why having an attitude of working for yourself first and the company second will put you in the driver's seat of your career. You learn how to be proactive, not reactive, as an independent contractor and seize opportunities in your place of employment that will benefit you, whether you remain with the company or not. In this section you learn exactly how to be on the offensive and in control, no matter what happens with the stability or instability of your employer. You don't have to be at anyone's mercy in an age of uncertainty and rapid changes. With the information in this chapter, you will be prepared for anything.

Strategy 8: Think National

In the past, many individuals traditionally grew their careers within a few miles of where they were born, went to school, and had their families and lifelong friends. There has been a growing shift away from this sort of micro living. Due to the downsizing of many of our local employers, there has been an increasing need for career-minded individuals to look nationwide for employment opportunities.

In this section you discover how thinking nationally will dramatically increase your odds of career success. Here you learn how to evaluate the *professional* advantages and drawbacks of a move to another part of the country. You learn also how to weigh the *personal* benefits and disadvantages. You learn how to open up communication with your family about the sensitive issues surrounding relocation. Key fears and barriers will be placed in perspective. You will discover how to research a new geographical market and how to write a plan to get your career and family from point A to point B both figuratively and physically. Before you rule out the option to think national, read this chapter with an open mind. You just may discover it is the best way to grow your career in the new economy and be better compensated than if you had remained local.

Strategy 9: Go Global

Worldwide hiring is up. During the second quarter of 1995, there was a 20 percent increase in international executive demand over the same time period in 1994. According to New York City based Korn/Ferry, executive demand escalated throughout Europe, Asia, and the United States. Richard M. Ferry, chairman and CEO of Korn/Ferry International states, "there is a growing confidence in the economy among global business leaders despite mixed signals in economic news." As the future belongs more and more to global business and international strategic alliances such as the 1990s version of the joint marketing of American Airlines and British Airways, opportunities for careers abroad will steadily increase.

This section helps you assess whether you are a candidate for a career abroad. You discover if you have the necessary skills and cross cultural mind-set to work in a foreign country. You learn how to analyze your motives and assess whether you are doing it for the right reasons. Your success depends on it.

In this section you also learn about the top growth regions of the world. You discover which industries are experiencing the most increases in demand for personnel abroad. This section covers the unique skills you need to work abroad and gives you global job-hunting tactics that can be put to work for you immediately.

Strategy 10: Start Your Own Business

When he was twenty-five, Jim had pennies in his pocket, no money in the bank, and creditors calling. Thirty years later, through self-discipline and hard work, he has become a self-made success story. "Either you design your future," says Jim, "or somebody else will design it for you."

Like many of us, Jim thought his inability to achieve financial independence was related to issues like the government, taxes, and competition. "My philosophy was all wrong," he states. "I was preventing myself from succeeding. We tend to blame whatever happens to us on those external things, but we need to take personal responsibility." This story appeared in *Entrepreneur*, January 1996, in the article "Just Do It" by Robert McGarvey.

A lot of studies have been done on how companies are moving more and more away from permanent jobs to temporary assignments and outsourcing. The information age will offer a vast array of possibilities for entrepreneurs. For many people, owning their own business will become the most practical way to remain permanently employed.

In this section you discover how to assess your entrepreneurial capabilities. Essentially, you learn if you have what it takes to start and run your own business. There are tips on starting your own business with little or no money and how to minimize your risks and losses. Whether or not you've ever considered owning your own business, this section will help you decide if the whole new world of being a small business owner is for you.

STRATEGY 1

Update Your Attitude

The ever-changing work environment can leave almost anyone in a state of fear, anxiety, and with a negative attiude. Before we can update our attitude and put fears and anxieties into perspective, we must first understand how we got to where we are today.

Job Insecurity

Rapid changes in business are making many workers vulnerable to pink slips, stagnation, and total disruption of their careers and financial lives. Even the job security once guaranteed to federal workers has ended. With the November and December 1995 shutdowns of the U.S. government, fear for job security became rampant in both the government and the private sector. With budget cuts looming for years to come, administration officials laid off 25,000 to 30,000 federal workers in 1996 alone.

Recent statistics from government and private health insurance plans indicate that mental health expenditures have been rising faster than any other medical benefit. "One explanation for the steady growth of mental health problems over the past twenty years is the increased pace, pressure, and uncertainty of modern business life," says Tim Davis in the March 1991 issue of *Business Horizons*. He states, "The 1970s and 1980s were marked by a great deal of social, economic, and technological change. A lot of companies went through retrenchments, downsizing, and restructuring. An unprecedented number of takeovers, mergers, and buyouts also took place during this period. The impact of all this on the individual employee has been very unsettling."

Much of the anxiety and negative attitudes that individuals may be feeling about the future, or even tension and depression in some cases, is undoubtedly due to the many pressures and uncertainties of the changing work environment. Many employees have been left in a state of shock as they have watched many of their colleagues terminated and discarded after years of dedication and loyal service to a company. For the dislocated worker, the anxiety has been great. However, the anxiety for those who have been left behind may be even greater as the fear of the corporate ax falling looms and builds tension in the ever-elusive future.

A nationwide survey of 350,000 employees conducted by Survey Research Corporation (ISR) in Chicago, reveals the percentage of respondents who frequently worry about being laid off has more than doubled over the past five years, from 20 percent in 1990 to 44 percent in 1995. Respondents who believe that hard-working employees can count on keeping their current jobs sharply declined from 69 percent in 1990 to 49 percent in 1994 and continues to fall. In fact, the more dedicated and loyal an employee is to the company, the more vulnerable he or she may be to states of worry, acute anxiety, tension, and even depression.

The 1990s have been the years when many businesses were forced to reduce their costs to remain competitive in the ever-complex, growing global economy. The deepest and most significant cuts were made in payroll. Continuous advances in technology and automation have fueled business's ability to reduce labor costs. For example, in 1985 IBM had 8,500 employees working at its center in Boca Raton, Florida. In January 1996, the office was operating with fewer than 1,000 employees.

The Victims

Those who are most likely to be the victims of the new economy and remain in a state of anxiety and perpetual fear are the middle managers and lower-level employees who continuously wonder whether they will be the next to be let go. Buyouts and hostile takeovers place this group of workers in an extremely vulnerable position. Senior managers, on the other hand, have had some protection with generous severance compensation that has helped minimize their fear and losses. Anxiety has been heightened for the middle managers and lower-level employees where mergers and acquisitions are poorly handled. Many companies, in their state of indecision and bad communication, leave employees in an unhealthy state of suspense for months and even years. Because of this, many workers wrestle with day-to-day insecurities, such as wondering who their next boss will be or if they will still have a job.

Most affected are fired managers who face long and deeply depressing job searches. For those over fifty, job loss is particularly devastating. For those entering their forties, the maturing of the baby-boom generation in the 1980s made competition fierce for a shrinking number of middle management jobs. The dislocations and disruptions in businesses going into the year 2000 have not only been a challenge to their ability to cope and survive, but for the individual as well.

Take the Stress Test

Psychologists believe that individuals who are stressed out about their jobs and careers get that way because they are in a situation in which they have little control. Stress will impact their attitude and outlook on life in a negative way. The feelings of anxiety and stress can be broken down into a sense of being powerless, incompetent (possibly because of all the new technology), and helpless. If you are experiencing any of the above symptoms, it may be beneficial to take the stress test to find out just how effectively you are coping with all the changes that have occurred in your world of work. Of course, keep in mind that stress in and of itself is not harmful. We all have felt stress before getting up in front of a group to speak. This type of stress can actually make us more energized and more effective at what we do. The following test will help you determine if your stress is bad or good. You will discover if your stress is helping you succeed or contributing to a possible bad attitude and ultimate defeat.

How Well Do You Handle Stress?

Rate yourself as to how you typically react in each of the situations listed:

Question	Always	Frequently	Sometimes	Never
1. Do you have the tendency to work on a deadline even if it means staying up into the middle of the night to complete it?	a	b	c	d
2. Do you thrive on situations in which there is pressure, competition, tension, and risk?	a	b	c	d
3. Do you find stress or tension has been a driving force behind many of your major accomplishments?	a	b	c	d
4. Do you feel exhilarated or energized after accomplishing a difficult task or closing an important business deal?	a	b	c	d
5. Do you enjoy novelty and challenge in your work?	a	b	c	d
6. Do you have a tendency to see obstacles as challenges rather than headaches?	a	b	c	d
7. Are you constantly seeking ways to improve yourself or your performance in your field?	a	b	c	d
8. In general, would you classify yourself as a risk-taker rather than a risk-avoider?	a	b	c	d
9. Are you willing to give up job security for job challenge?	a	b	c	d
10. Are you able to "come down" physically and emotionally a few hours after a tension-producing event?	a	b	c	d
11. Do you seek action-oriented vacations?	a	b	c	d

Circle One Per Question

	Circle One Per Question			
Question	Always	Frequently	Sometimes	Never
12. In your leisure time do you pursue activities in which there is a certain amount of challenge or risk (i.e., rock climbing)?	a	b	c	d

Scoring	4=a	3=b	2=c	1=d	Total=	Total=	Total=	Total=

TOTAL SCORE:_____

Answer Key: Add up your total by using the scoring above.
　36–48: You are a true handler of stress and direct it in a positive way in your life. You enjoy challenges and excitement in work and leisure.
　24–35: You probably like to balance status quo with some change and risk to stay on an even keel.
　12–23: You are likely to avoid stress, avoid facing change, and delay confronting difficult issues in your life and career.

A Positive Attitude Drives a Winning Career

How, in the midst of all this upheaval, can an individual change his or her attitude from a negative to positive one? Why is a positive update of one's attitude even important? Terry Bowden, Auburn University's head football coach, proved that a positive attitude could help drive a college football team to an 11–0 season in his first year as head coach. He also has personally discovered and believes that a positive attitude can help drive a successful career. "Getting a job," he states, in the March 6, 1994, issue of the Rocky Mountain News, "is competing, just like sports. In football, the winning team is not always the biggest, the strongest, or the fastest. It is often the team that believes that it can win, regardless of the competition. Your career is no different. Winning has everything to do with your positive attitude, and your persistence. If you believe you can, and should win you will find success."

Fear Is Self-Defeating

My last book, *The Top 10 Fears of Job Seekers*, discussed how fear and anxiety hamper our quest for career success. It is self-defeating. Essentially, winners do not have the luxury or the time to dwell on their fears. In the book I state, "Fear puts our quest for success in reverse. As a result, we shield ourselves from rejection, make fewer contacts, and avoid result-oriented activities. . . . The results of fear range from an inability to network and make contacts, to being unable to sell oneself effectively."

Face Change Head-On

Instead of having a bad attitude and worrying about all the changes that are so rapidly taking place, as we discussed earlier in this chapter, face them head-on. Look at them straight in the eye and say, "I am better than you. Nothing is going to stop me from succeeding." In the introduction, we discussed how there are two ways to manage change: fight or flight. By facing reality, and facing it head-on, you have decided to fight. Now you are being proactive and not reactive. You have chosen to channel your anxiety into a positive force and demonstrate a will to win.

One way to face the future is to accept the new values of the future workplace and make a commitment to change and develop yourself with them. Be determined to find out how you can help your current and future employers to meet their most immediate needs. Continually look for newer and better ways to be of more value to your employers. Deliver what they currently want: increased profits, reduced costs, better productivity, efficiency, more sales, and much, much more. If you can shift your thinking and embrace these values, you will have an attitude that will be of more value to any company in the future economy and you will remain highly marketable.

Turn Stress into Survival

Shift your thinking to turn stress into survival. "Don't keep yourself stuck in an information vacuum," writes Sander Marcus in the March 1993 issue of *Society for Human Resource Management HR Magazine*. Decide to be a survivor and get informed. Instead of being stressed out, he encourages career-minded individuals to get the latest information on the ever-changing world. "Too many who did a good job fifteen or twenty years ago are today doing the same thing and thinking that they are still doing a good job. If this is you, you're in for a shock. Your company has changed; you need to change with it."

No longer can any worker justify being uninformed about what is happening in his or her company, industry, country, or even the world. Keep in mind that a factory or an industry change in a country far away may have a direct impact on your job or career. You need to be tuned in to the latest information concerning your career and industry. Sander Marcus writes, "Without accurate and timely information, you are guessing, and this is an economy in which you cannot afford to guess."

Ten Action Steps to Update Your Attitude

Here are ten action steps that you can implement right now. With these steps, you can immediately update your attitude and channel your stress into a positive force for your life and future career.

1. *Take responsibility for yourself.* Stop blaming others for your situation. Deal with the world the way it is, not the way you wish it to be.

2. *Make time for reflection.* Engage in periods of quiet time. For instance, even when you're driving in the car or commuting on a train or flight, focus on what you have achieved and appreciate your family and friends who support you on a daily basis and are there for you. Think positive thoughts.

3. *Exercise.* Exercise renews your attitude about your life and career. You'll get a brain chemical called endorphin spinning around in your head. It has a similar chemical makeup to the drug Valium, and it's cheaper, too.

4. *Discuss your fears, worries, and concerns with others you can trust.* This is important because when we open up and talk with others, we gain the value of collective brainstorming and helpful feedback.

5. *Discuss your career and future with a qualified therapist or career counselor.* They have testing programs and insights that will help you focus on your strengths and identify where you need to improve.

6. *Establish a to-do list.* Write down the areas of your career and life that most need improving to get ready for the future now.

Instead of having a negative attitude about it, do something about it.

7. *Agree on a time frame when you wish to have your to-do list completed.* Without a time frame commitment—well, you know what will happen.

8. *Subscribe to two or three major newspapers and magazines.* Make a commitment to reading and being informed. Stop living in a vacuum.

9. *Learn something new at work.* Involve yourself on a task force or volunteer for additional on-the-job or classroom training, and don't expect to get paid for it. Do it for your own career growth.

10. *Dress like a winner.* Update your business wardrobe with an outfit or two. Even if you haven't achieved complete competency in your attitude and skills, acting like you have goes a long way in creating a better attitude.

STRATEGY 2

Discover the Future Growth Industries

Here is an introduction to a world of exciting fields, industries, and companies that will inhabit the year 2000 and beyond. It is an opening to an exciting world of new jobs. In some cases, it will guide you in the direction of jobs that don't even have names yet.

Two Shifts

In general, the new jobs can be summarized in two dramatic shifts from the past. The first is a shift from a twentieth-century, manufacturing-based economy to a twenty-first-century, service-producing economy. DRI/McGraw-Hill reports in the November 15, 1995, issue of *The Atlanta Constitution* that in the state of Georgia alone, "manufacturing in 1955 represented 35% of the

21

state's employment opportunities. By the year 2005, it is estimated that it will represent less than 15%. In 1955 service represented 10%. It is estimated by the year 2005 service will be nearly 30%."

The second shift is a change in emphasis from white-collar, professionally based jobs to computer-oriented, technically based jobs. In fact, some researchers predict that by the turn of the century, eight of ten jobs will not require a bachelor's degree. Technical jobs, many of which are still emerging, will be the fastest growing segment of the new world of work. It is predicted that these jobs will offer salaries competitive with current white-collar professional pay scales.

In order to keep up, thinking will have to shift as well. Previous definitions of career success will need to be reassessed. The old drumbeat of having to be a doctor or lawyer to have a sense of honor and fulfillment is very limiting. Social status will be redefined not by education but by the ability to adapt to technology and contribute to society in a rapidly changing information age. Employers will increasingly favor not those with advanced graduate degrees but those with four-year degrees and technical expertise and those with two-year technical degrees. A four-year liberal arts college degree will not become a thing of the past, but knowledge of technology will be the key factor in the hiring processes of most corporations.

Small Business Is Where It's At

In considering the future growth industries, fields, and companies, it is important to realize that the small business sector is where it is all happening. Daily, new businesses are starting up to meet the needs of the future. In many cases it will be new, small businesses that will rise to the challenge of finding an emerging futuristic need and filling it. After all, it is the unique ability of small business to move quickly on an idea and innovate and implement many times faster than their large, bureaucratic counterparts.

If you take a job with a cutting-edge small business, it is probable that you could become wealthy through the company's stock options alone. Getting involved with an innovative small business could have more long-term financial rewards than any short-term salary you could earn from any employer.

The location of new and small businesses is changing, too. "Instead of being in traditional centers of industry and finance such as Chicago, Detroit, Los Angeles, and New York, industrial centers seem to be shifting rapidly. Small businesses are reshuffling the country's economic deck," states Carol Kleiman, syndicated career columnist and author. Through her research, the following patterns can be found: High-technology firms are booming in Seattle; telemarketing companies in central regions like Omaha, Nebraska; financial services in Salt Lake City; insurance in Des Moines; supercomputers in Minneapolis; industrial exports in Peoria, Illinois; franchises in Wichita; sports equipment in Indianapolis; computer software in Columbus, Ohio; health care in Louisville, Kentucky; restaurants in Portland, Maine; credit cards in Wilmington, Delaware; and tourism in Orlando, Florida.

The Exciting Possibilities

To help you quickly learn where the future jobs, industries, fields, and companies will be, the following tables have been compiled for you. The tables have been placed in an easy-to-read format, based on the research of Carol Kleiman, author of *The 100 Best Jobs for the 1990s and Beyond*, A. David Silver, author of *Quantum Companies*, and the U.S. Bureau of Labor and Statistics. The following information creates exciting possibilities for any individual who wants to become a winner in the next century.

The Top Six Growth Fields

A Prospect of Growing Fields

Listed below are six fields showing promise of future growth potential into the twenty-first century.

1. **Health Care**
   Technology will continue to create new breakthroughs in patient treatments. Revolutions in health care will continually create new opportunities at all employment levels.

2. **Robotics**
   Experts project a new generation of robots that can see, hear, feel, and obey. The demand for engineers, technicians, installers, and repair people will steadily increase.

3. **Computer Graphics**
   CAD (computer-aided design) and CAI (computer-aided imagery) will be two of the

24

fastest-growing fields into the year 2000 and beyond. They will revolutionize design in manufacturing, fashion, film, and video.

4. Information Technology

Advances in telecommunications, fiber optics, mega communication mergers, and the Internet all make for an explosion of jobs in this fast-growing field.

5. Biotechnology

Solving medical problems with the new technology is the new frontier into the next century. Individuals with backgrounds in science, biology, engineering, and chemistry will have unlimited opportunities in this field into the next century.

6. Lasers

They will be used in a variety of ways ranging from health care and communications to manufacturing. For individuals in these fields who have laser knowledge, opportunities will remain plentiful.

Source: U.S. Bureau of Labor and Statistics

The 100 Best Jobs Going into the Next Century

Our changing world has dictated the best jobs going into the next century. For example, seventy-six million baby boomers will be in their fifties. The graying population will open new demands in health care, retirement-related industries, and travel and leisure. Jobs will be further influenced by the information technology explosion and new breakthroughs in genetics, bioengineering, robotics, and environmental research. Further influences will be the fact that women, minorities, and immigrants will account for 80 percent of the U.S. labor force growth. White men, who for decades were the majority, will make up only 15 percent of new entrants into the workforce. Based on these and a variety of other factors, the following table represents the 100 best jobs going into the next century.

25

The 100 Best Jobs

(In Alphabetical Order)

Accountant/auditor
Actor/director/producer
Advertising and marketing account
  supervisor
Agricultural scientist
Aircraft technician
Appliance/power tool repairer
Architect
Arts administrator
Automotive mechanic
Bank loan officer
Bank marketer
Carpenter
Chemist
Clerical supervisor/office manager
Commercial/graphic artists
Computer operator
Computer programmer
Computer service technician
Computer systems analyst
Cook/chef
Corporate financial analyst
Corporate personnel trainer
Corrections officer/guard/jailer
Cosmetologist
Court reporter
Database manager
Dental hygienist
Dentist
Drafter
Economist
Editor/writer
Educational administrator
Employment interviewer
Engineer
Environmental scientist
Farm manager
Financial planner
Firefighter

Flight attendant
Flight engineer
Food scientist
Health services administrator
Home health aide
Hotel manager/assistant
Human resources manager/executive
Industrial designer
Information systems manager
Insurance claim examiner
Insurance salesperson
Interior designer
Investment banker
Labor relations specialist
Landscape architect
Lawyer
Librarian
Licensed practical nurse
Management consultant
Manufacturing specialist (CAD, CAM and
  CAI)
Manager
Mathematician/statistician
Medical records administrator
Occupational therapist
Office/business machine repairer
Operations manager/manufacturing
Operations/systems research analyst
Ophthalmic laboratory technician
Optician
Paralegal
Paramedic
Peripheral electronic data processing
  equipment operator
Pharmacist
Photographer/camera operator
Physical therapist
Physician
Physician's assistant

Physicist/astronomer

Pilot

Podiatrist

Police officer

Psychologist/counselor

Public relations specialist

Radio/TV news reporter

Radio/TV service technician

Radiologic technologist

Real estate agent/broker

Real estate appraiser

Registered nurse

Reporter/correspondent

Restaurant/food service

Retail salesperson

Secretary/administrator

Social worker

Speech pathologist/audiologist

Teacher/professor

Travel agent

Truck driver

Underwriter

Veterinarian

Wholesale sales representative

The 100 Future Growth Companies

Perhaps equally important as the 100 best jobs are 100 companies that epitomize how the business world is going to look in the next century. These companies represent the future career opportunities and the overall dramatic changes that will impact every aspect of our lives. A. David Silver, in his book *Quantum Companies,* has uncovered 100 companies that are poised to deliver the future aggressively. They include a diverse range such as environmental services, health care delivery, trucking, connectivity hardware, education, telephony, computer software, facilities management, organ transplantation, and companies with high social utility. He states, "Many of the Quantum 100 companies are focused on improving the global village. You'll find a company that destroys hazardous materials and creates basic elements that can be reused by industry; another manages public schools; and a company that makes a building material that is stronger than oak out of soybeans and old newsprint."

This next table provides you with the information you need to consider taking a job with one of these growth companies or with a similar one. It gives you criteria in order to evaluate other companies that may have similar possibilities, growth, and market leadership essential to an exciting career in the next century. These 100 companies are not meant to limit your vision but to act as a forecast as to what is ahead. Keep in mind that some of the companies have headquarters in other countries; however, they do maintain operations in the United States. For that matter, many of the companies listed operate in other locations throughout the United States.

The 100 Future Growth Companies

Name	Type of Business	Address
1. Acxiom Corporation	Designs, develops, produces, markets, and supports computer systems for the direct mail and telemarketing industry	301 Industrial Blvd. Conway, AK 72032
2. American Medical Response, Inc.	A consolidator of ambulance companies	67 Batterymarch St. Boston, MA 02110
3. Asante Technologies, Inc.	Designs, produces, markets, and supports data networking products, particularly for Macintosh Ethernet adapters	821 Fox Lane San Jose, CA 95131
4. Ascend Communications, Inc.	Develops, produces, markets, and supports a broad range of digital wide area network access products	1275 Harbor Bay Parkway Alameda, CA 94502

Source: Reprinted by permission of Peterson's, Princeton, NJ 08543, from *Quantum Companies II* by A. David Slater © 1996 by the author. Available at local bookstores or by calling the publisher at 1-800-338-3282.

Discover the Future Growth Industries

Name	Type of Business	Address
5. Atmel Corporation	Designs, develops, and manufactures high-performance memory and logic chips for telecommunications and other markets	2125 O'Nel Dr. San Jose, CA 95131
6. Bay Networks, Inc.	A technology leader in Internet working computer systems that connect LANs to WANs	8 Federal Street Billerica, MA 01821
7. Better Education, Inc.	Develops, produces, and markets an interactive student computer instructional system to let the teacher know when the student is not understanding something	4822 George Washington Blvd. Yorktown, VA 23692
8. The Body Shop International, Inc.	Develops, produces, and sells cosmetics and skin and hair products based on natural ingredients	Watersmead Littlehampton West Sussex, UK BN176LS
9. Cambridge Neuroscience, Inc.	The discovery and development of proprietary pharmaceutical products to treat severe neurological and psychiatric disorders	1 Kendall Square Cambridge, MA 02139
10. Cambridge Technology Partners	Provides software development and information systems consulting services in the complicated transition to next-generation open and distributed computing	304 Vassar St. Cambridge, MA 02139

Source: Reprinted by permission of Peterson's, Princeton, NJ 08543, from *Quantum Companies II* by A. David Slater © 1996 by the author. Available at local bookstores or by calling the publisher at 1-800-338-3282.

The Top 10 Career Strategies

Name	Type of Business	Address
11. Catalina Marketing Corporation	Provides cost-effective methods of implementing a targeted consumer marketing strategy based on an electronic company system	11300 Ninth St. N St. Petersburg, FL 33716
12. C-Cube Microsystems Inc.	Provides products and solutions to permit videos to be transmitted over desktop PCs and direct-broadcast satellite systems	1778 McCarthy Blvd. Milpitas, CA 95035
13. Cerner Corporation	Creates patient information monitoring systems that account for every patient and all of his or her costs, admission to discharge	2800 Rockcreek Pkwy. Kansas City, MO 64117
14. Chipcom Corporation	Designs, develops, and manufactures computer switching hubs and other networking products	118 Turnpike Rd. Southborough, MA 01772
15. Cirrus Logic, Inc.	Develops integrated circuits for applications such as graphics, audio, video, and communications data acquisition and mass storage	3100 W. Warren Ave. Fremont, CA 94538
16. Computer Network Technology Corp.	Designs, develops, and manufactures networking products linking remote dissimilar computing platforms and enables them to communicate easily	6500 Wedgwood Rd. Maple Grove, MN 55311
17. Corel Corporation	A leading publisher of graphics and small computer interface software; owns WordPerfect products	1600 Carling Ave. Ottawa, Ontario, CAN K1Z8R7

Source: Reprinted by permission of Peterson's, Princeton, NJ 08543, from *Quantum Companies II* by A. David Slater © 1996 by the author. Available at local bookstores or by calling the publisher at 1-800-338-3282.

Discover the Future Growth Industries

Name	Type of Business	Address
18. Corrections Corporation of America	The largest private owner/ operator of prisons in the United States	102 Woodmont Blvd. Nashville, TN 37027
19. Davidson & Associates, Inc.	The leading publisher of educational software in the World (Their retail product Mathblaster has sold more than 1.5 million copies)	19840 Pioneer Ave. Torrance, CA 90503
20. Decision Quest	Serves litigants, predicting jury trial verdicts and developing trial strategies	2050 W. 190th St. Torrance, CA 90504
21. Digital Link Corp.	Designs, manufactures, and markets data communications products for wide-area networks	217 Humboldt Sunnyvale, CA 94089
22. Dionex Corporation	Designs, develops, and manufactures systems used in environmental monitoring and in regulating the chemical composition of food, beverages, and cosmetics	1228 Titan Way Sunnyvale, CA 94088
23. DNX Corporation	The leader of transplanting animal organs into humans	303B College Rd. E Princeton, NJ 08540
24. Ecoscience Corp.	Discovers and develops natural pest control products; develops coatings to extend the shelf life of fruits and vegetables	3 Biotech Park Worcester, MA 01605
25. Education Alternatives, Inc.	The leader in the private management of schools	7900 Xerxes Ave. S Minneapolis, MN 55431

Source: Reprinted by permission of Peterson's, Princeton, NJ 08543, from *Quantum Companies II* by A. David Slater © 1996 by the author. Available at local bookstores or by calling the publisher at 1-800-338-3282.

Name	Type of Business	Address
26. ENSYS Environmental Products, Inc.	Develops on-site user-friendly kits to detect environmental contaminants	4222 Emperor Blvd. Morrisville, NC 27560
27. Envirotest Systems Corp.	The leading provider of centralized vehicle-emissions testing programs for states and municipalities	2002 N. Forbes Blvd. Tucson, AZ 85745
28. Fore Systems, Inc.	Designs, develops, manufactures, and sells high-performance networking products based on ATM technology	174 Thorn Hill Rd. Warrendale, PA 15086
29. Frontier Insurance Group, Inc.	Underwriter and creator of specialty insurance products that serve markets that are considered unattractive and have few competitors	195 Lake Louise Marie Rd. Rock Hill, NY 12775
30. GTI Corporation	The leading supplier of magnetic components for signal processing and power transfer functions in networking products	9171 Centre Dr. San Diego, CA 92122
31. Harmony Brook, Inc.	Manufactures and sells equipment that processes tap water into high-quality drinking water at point of use	1030 Lone Oak Rd. Egan, MN 55121
32. Hauser Chemical Research, Inc.	Produces life-saving and life-enhancing products from natural sources, many of them found in forests	5555 Airport Blvd. Boulder, CO 80301
33. Health Management Associates, Inc.	The leading provider of nonurban medical hospitals located in the Southeast and Southwest	5811 Pelican Bay Blvd. Naples, FL 33963

Source: Reprinted by permission of Peterson's, Princeton, NJ 08543, from *Quantum Companies II* by A. David Slater © 1996 by the author. Available at local bookstores or by calling the publisher at 1-800-338-3282.

Discover the Future Growth Industries

Name	Type of Business	Address
34. Healthdyne Technologies, Inc.	Produces a microprocessor to monitor people at sleep and intervene in sudden infant death syndrome and various adult illnesses	1255 Kennestone Circle Marietta, GA 30066
35. Heart Technology	Manufactures a "plaque buster" that pulverizes plaque in persons with coronary artery disease	17425 N.E. Union Hill Rd. Redmond, WA 98052
36. Hemosol Associates, Inc.	Develops an artificial red blood cell substitute, mainly for persons with blood-borne infectious diseases such as hepatitis and AIDS	115 Skyway Ave. Etibicoke, CAN M9W 4Z4
37. Homecare Management, Inc.	Provides home care to patients who have undergone organ transplants	80 Air Park Dr. Ronkonkoma, NY 11779
38. Information America, Inc.	The leading provider of on-line services for the banking and legal industries	1 Georgia Ctr. Atlanta, GA 30308
39. Informix Corporation	Designs, produces, and supports software for client servers and database management	4100 Bohannon Dr. Menlo Park, CA 94025
40. Integrated Health Services, Inc.	Buys, operates, and upgrades geriatric facilities to provide care equal to hospitals but at 30 to 60 percent less	10065 Red Run Blvd. Owings Mill, MD 21117
41. International High Tech Marketing, Inc.	International distributor of PCs and related products to developing countries	12285 S.W. 129th Ct. Miami, FL 33186

Source: Reprinted by permission of Peterson's, Princeton, NJ 08543, from *Quantum Companies II* by A. David Slater © 1996 by the author. Available at local bookstores or by calling the publisher at 1-800-338-3282.

The Top 10 Career Strategies

Name	Type of Business	Address
42. Invision Systems Corporation	Develops and supports software that brings full-motion video to PCs attached to networks	8500 Leesburg Pike Vienna, VA 22182
43. Just for Feet, Inc.	Operates superstores that specialize in brand-name athletic and outdoor footwear	3000 Riverchase Galleria Birmingham, AL 35244
44. Landstar Systems, Inc.	Operates trucking companies that create independent business opportunities for thousands of drivers	1000 Bridgeport Ave. Shelton, CT 06484
45. Life Resuscitation Technologies, Inc.	Researches and develops organ resuscitation technologies to reduce brain and other organ damage from oxygen deprivation	2434 N. Greenview Ave. Chicago, IL 60614
46. Medicenter, Inc.	Offers facilities management of health care options to large employers	13 N.W. Forty-fourth St. Lawton, OK 73505
47. Medicus Systems Corp.	Develops and supports information management systems used by physicians, nurses, and administrators in the health care industry	1 Rotary Ctr. Evanston, IL 60201
48. Medrad, Inc.	Develops, manufactures, and markets products that enhance medical images of the human body	271 Kappa Dr. Pittsburgh, PA 15238
49. Megahertz Holding Corp.	A leading manufacturer of data/ fax modems for the mobile computing industry	4505 S. Wasatch Blvd. Salt Lake City, UT 84124

Source: Reprinted by permission of Peterson's, Princeton, NJ 08543, from *Quantum Companies II* by A. David Slater © 1996 by the author. Available at local bookstores or by calling the publisher at 1-800-338-3282.

Discover the Future Growth Industries

Name	Type of Business	Address
50. Mitek Surgical Products, Inc.	Leading supplier of minimally invasive surgical implants	57 Providence Hwy. Norwood, MA 02062
51. Molten Metal Technology	Produces a waste disposal system that transforms toxic materials into harmless basic materials	51 Sawyer Rd. Waltham, MA 02154
52. Mothers Work, Inc.	The leading specialty retailer of upscale maternity clothes	1309 Noble St. Philadelphia, PA 19123
53. National Health Corp.	Offers affordable health insurance to the self-employed and small-business owners	1901 N. State Hwy. 360 Grand Prairie, TX 75070
54. NetFrame Systems, Inc.	Specializes in superservers for linking PCs in local area networks	1545 Barber La. Milipitas, CA 95035
55. Neurogen Corp.	Capitalizes on advances in neuroscience and molecular biology to develop pharmaceuticals for brain disorders	35 N.E. Industrial Rd. Branford, CT 06405
56. Newbridge Networks Corp.	Supplies equipment for worldwide communications networks	600 March Rd. Kanata, Ontario, CAN K2K 2E6
57. Nextel Communications, Inc.	Currently building the lowest-cost digital cellular network to compete with AT&T	201 Rt. 17 N Rutherford, NJ 07070
58. On Assignment, Inc.	Leader in the rent-a-chemist field	26651 W. Agoura Rd. Calabasas, CA 91302
59. Orbital Sciences Corp.	Private ownership and operation of orbiting satellites	21700 Atlantic Blvd. Dulles, VA 20166

Source: Reprinted by permission of Peterson's, Princeton, NJ 08543, from *Quantum Companies II* by A. David Slater © 1996 by the author. Available at local bookstores or by calling the publisher at 1-800-338-3282.

The Top 10 Career Strategies

Name	Type of Business	Address
60. Orthogene, Inc.	Offers genetically engineered solutions to bone, joint, and other cartilage diseases	2330 Marinship Way Sausalito, CA 94965
61. Parametric Technology Corp.	Develops and supports software that automates mechanical design through the manufacturing process	128 Technology Dr. Waltham, MA 02154
62. Parcplace Systems, Inc.	Develops and supports software that corresponds to real-world business relationships; helps companies with management structures and internal communications	999 E. Arques Ave. Sunnyvale, CA 94086
63. Phenix Biocomposites, Inc.	Produces a building material that looks like granite and acts like wood, but is made of soybeans and used newspapers	1511 Gault St. St. Peter, MN 56082
64. Pleasant Company	Produces books, dolls, and accessories that educate young girls about different periods of American history	8400 Fairway Pl. Middleton, WI 53562
65. The Progressive Corp.	Underwrites property and casualty insurance for people canceled or rejected by others	6300 Wilson Mills Rd. Mayfield Village, OH 44143
66. Qualcomm, Inc.	Leader in digital wireless technologies	6455 Lusk Bvd. San Diego, CA 92121
67. Quantum Health Resources, Inc.	Provides therapy and support services for patients affected by chronic disorders requiring lifelong therapy	790 The City Drive S Orange, CA 92668

Source: Reprinted by permission of Peterson's, Princeton, NJ 08543, from *Quantum Companies II* by A. David Slater © 1996 by the author. Available at local bookstores or by calling the publisher at 1-800-338-3282.

Discover the Future Growth Industries

Name	Type of Business	Address
68. Quorum Health Group, Inc.	Manages hospitals in forty-four states; continues to grow by acquiring inefficiently run 100-to-400 bed hospitals in medium-sized markets	155 Franklin Rd. Brentwood, TN 37027
69. Res-Care, Inc.	Provides residences and support to mentally handicapped people	1300 Embassy Sq. Louisville, KY 40299
70. Research Management Consultants, Inc.	Provides technical and scientific consulting services to government agencies and technology-driven corporations	601 Daily Dr. Camarillo, CA 93010
71. Roper Industries, Inc.	Produces heavy-duty oil and gas field pumping equipment; has a client base in Russia	160 Ben Burton Rd. Bogart, GA 30622
72. Ryka, Inc.	Designs and markets athletic shoes specially designed for women's feet	249 Ocean Way Norwood, MA 02062
73. Sentinel Systems, Inc.	A leading distributor of home alarm and automation systems	2713 Magruder Blvd. Hampton, VA 23666
74. Shaman Pharmaceuticals, Inc.	Seeks out native plants in South American rain forests that may provide new medicinal drugs	213 E. Grand Ave. South San Francisco, CA 94080
75. SRX, Inc.	Develops and markets equipment that links telephone features with PCs and workstations	3480 Lotus Dr. Plano, TX 75075
76. Stores Automated Systems, Inc.	Customizes hardware and software solutions for supermarkets both for point-of-sale and store management	311 Sinclair St. Bristol, PA 19007

Source: Reprinted by permission of Peterson's, Princeton, NJ 08543, from *Quantum Companies II* by A. David Slater © 1996 by the author. Available at local bookstores or by calling the publisher at 1-800-338-3282.

Name	Type of Business	Address
77. Sunrise Medical, Inc.	Develops and manufactures products that permit the elderly and disabled to live at home and participate in their communities	2355 Crenshaw Blvd. Torrance, CA 90501
78. Swift Transportation Co, Inc.	One-day product delivery to clients like retailers; handles large shipments similarly to overnight package carriers	1705 Marietta Way Sparks, NY 89431
79. Sybase, Inc.	Develops and supports software for integrated and company-wide information management systems	6475 Christie Ave. Emeryville, CA 94608
80. Synaptic Pharmaceutical Corp.	Conducts research involving a chemical in the brain called serotonin	215 College Rd. Paramus, NJ 07652
81. Synopsys, Inc.	Offers integrated circuit software to speed up integrated circuits and electronic systems	700 E. Middlefield Rd. Mountain View, CA 94043
82. Systemix, Inc.	A biotechnology company developing universal donor cells to combat autoimmune disorders	3155 Porter Rd. Palo Alto, CA 94304
83. Tecnol Medical Products, Inc.	Designs and manufactures disposable medical products including surgical masks and back supports	7201 Industrial Park Blvd. Fort Worth, TX 76180
84. Tetra Tech, Inc.	Solves complex environmental cleanup and contamination problems	670 N. Rosemead Blvd. Pasadena, CA 91107

Discover the Future Growth Industries

Name	Type of Business	Address
85. Thermo Electron Corp.	Identifies emerging societal problems and develops technological solutions in spun-off subsidiary companies	81 Wyman St. Waltham, MA 02254
86. 3Com Corp.	Develops, sells, and supports global data networking systems	5400 Bayfront Plaza Santa Clara, CA 95052
87. Three-Five Systems, Inc.	Manufactures LED and LCD display devices for consumer electronic devices	10230 S. Fiftieth Pl. Phoenix, AZ 85044
88. Transmedia Network, Inc.	Issues membership cards giving consumers a 25 percent discount at participating restaurants	11900 Biscayne Blvd. North Miami, FL 33181
89. Tresp Associates, Inc.	Manages the data-processing operation of the federal government	4900 Seminary Rd. Alexandria, VA 22311
90. Vivra, Inc.	Owns and operates dialysis centers and has expanded into other rehabilitation therapies	400 Primrose Burlingame, CA 94010
91. Vivus	Developed a painless therapy for the treatment of male impotence and erectile dysfunction	545 Middlefield Rd. Menlo Park, CA 94025
92. Wall Data, Inc.	Develops and supports Windows-based software to enable PCs to communicate with mainframes and local and wide area networks	17769 N.E. Seventy-eighth Pl. Redmond, WA 98052
93. Whole Foods Market, Inc.	Owns and operates the nation's largest chain of natural foods supermarkets	2525 Wallingwood Dr. Austin, TX 78746

Source: Reprinted by permission of Peterson's, Princeton, NJ 08543, from *Quantum Companies II* by A. David Slater © 1996 by the author. Available at local bookstores or by calling the publisher at 1-800-338-3282.

Name	Type of Business	Address
94. Wholesome & Hearty Foods, Inc.	Produces food products that are meatless, soy-free, cholesterol-free, and low in fat	2422 S.E. Hawthorne Blvd. Portland, OR 97214
95. Work/Family Directions	Consults with corporations to put together work/family-related programs	930 Commonwealth Ave. Boston, MA 02215
96. Workstation Technologies, Inc.	Delivers high-quality video conferencing on a desktop computer, at low cost	18010 Sky Park Circle Irvine, CA 92714
97. Xilinx, Inc.	Designs and markets programmable logic integrated circuits	2100 Logic Dr. San Jose, CA 95124
98. Xircom, Inc.	Leading provider of products connecting laptop computers to LANs	26025 Mureau Rd. Calabrass, CA 91302
99. Zebra Technologies Corp.	Design and manufacture bar-code labeling systems for manufacturers to improve production control	333 Corporate Woods Parkway Vernon Hills, IL 60601
100. ZIA Metalurgical Processes, Inc.	Develops a steel-making process that is less expensive and produces a higher quality material	5344 Alpha Rd. Dallas, TX 75240

Source: Reprinted by permission of Peterson's, Princeton, NJ 08543, from *Quantum Companies II* by A. David Slater © 1996 by the author. Available at local bookstores or by calling the publisher at 1-800-338-3282.

Continue to Expand Your Knowledge

I hope reading about the companies listed above has enlarged your vision of the future and the multitude of new opportunities that are available to you. However, this is only the beginning. Continue expanding your knowledge of potential future cutting-edge employers through a number of resources. Here is a partial list:

Read as often as possible the following:

The Wall Street Journal
Business Week
Money
Forbes
Success
U.S. News and World Report
Fortune
Newsweek
Time

Read weekly the Sunday and Business Monday editions of the following:

The New York Times
The Los Angeles Times
Your local newspaper
The newspaper of the area where you would like to relocate someday

Remember, information gives you power. Make a commitment today to constantly expand your information base and learn something new daily. Don't worry about the one, two, and three dollars each of these journals may cost you at the point of purchase. If you get one tip, one lead, the money spent could produce a return on investment well beyond any dollar amount you could ever imagine.

STRATEGY 3

Develop the Right Skills

A school district in Florida preparing its students for the future was featured in a May 15, 1995 article in *The Orlando Sentinel*. The paper ran the following headline: "A Proposed Restructuring Of Curriculum Would Emphasize That All Students Be Versed in Teamwork, Flexibility and Critical Thinking." The article goes on to explain that in the past forty years not much has changed in education. Students still learn algebra, read Shakespeare, dissect frogs, study foreign languages, and memorize chemical formulas. In reality, however, only a small percentage of students will make use of this information and continue on for higher degrees. It states, "Out in the workplace, meanwhile, employers are looking for skills from every employee that once were thought to be limited to college graduates: teamwork, flexibility, critical thinking, adaptability and knowing how to learn."

The Soft Skills

Teamwork is one of the many soft skills emphasized by business as essential to the new work environment. By soft skills I mean those skills that are psychological and not related to the technical, or hard skills of our jobs. Later on in this section we will also explore the hard skills needed to be successful in the future.

Why are teamwork and other soft skills gaining so much notoriety? Throughout most of the twentieth century, in an industrial economy, the workforce was trained to do a single job and do it well. The worker was trained to work independently. The job skills that yesterday were critical are today, almost overnight, obsolete. Employees no longer are engaged independently in operating heavy machinery; they now work as a team to program and monitor the computers that operate the machines.

For skills to remain competitive in the future, successful individuals must stay ahead and seek ways to sharpen their skills for the new work environment. *Money* magazine, in March 1995, interviewed more than two dozen management consultants, human resource executives, corporate recruiters, and job counselors. Their unanimous advice: " Finely tuned skills like networking, and strategic planning are as important as ever, but the workplace of tomorrow demands even deeper, more elusive talents. Key job skills for the future include an ongoing appetite for change, ease with fast decision-making, and the ability to manage and motivate yourself." Here are twelve buzzwords that best describe the soft skills employers are looking for in the future worker:

- Teamwork
- Communication
- Initiative
- Vision
- Problem solving
- Adaptability
- Passion for change
- Fast decision-making
- Innovation
- Creativity
- Organization
- Leadership

The challenge, of course, is to acquire these soft skills. How do you learn or improve upon them? Mastering these skills is especially critical if you have not already sharpened them or made them a substantial and valid part of your résumé.

Ten Action Steps to Improve Soft Skills

Here are ten action steps you can take to make sure you are entering the future world of work with the training and experience in the necessary soft skills:

1. *Cross-train.* Cross-train within the company and position you currently hold. Try other jobs in other departments, even if it means volunteering on your own free time. The more you know about the company, the greater an asset you become and the

more you are considered a team player. Promotions and job security for you will be virtually guaranteed.

2. *Start a task force or participate in one.* A task force is a great place to learn team-based work skills. It will also help you learn how to generate creativity and innovation in your work style. It will get you thinking beyond your current job and help you to look at the company as a whole.

3. *Initiate new ideas and improvements.* We all talk about an island on the distant horizon. We call it "Someday I'll." Increase your soft skills by implementing some of those projects you've been wanting to do but keep putting off by saying, "Someday I'll . . ." By attacking new projects, you'll develop the ability to take action, initiate, develop creativity, and much more. Besides benefiting the company, you'll take the experience and skills you've developed and make them part of your résumé and increase your marketability.

4. *Ask questions frequently.* Develop your communication skills by learning to ask questions more frequently. Don't act like you know it all, even if you think you do. People who ask questions are perceived more intelligently than those who don't.

5. *Confront coworkers and bosses on tough issues.* Rand, a manager of a major hotel, confronted the manager of another department with her less than cooperative working relationship with his department. His suggestion was, "Let's learn to get along with each other and even cross-train in each other's department." His suggestion helped both of them learn other areas of the operation, get along better, create teamwork, and make them each more successful. It worked. They each were promoted in less than a year.

6. *Enroll in the next company-sponsored seminar or work-*

shop. Many companies offer a wide variety of soft skill training workshops. Talk to your human resources department. You will discover classroom and video-based training programs on subjects like teamwork, communication, leadership, time management, and much more. The next time you are invited to company-sponsored training, go and do it for yourself. It could have cost you hundreds of dollars at a university. It's free at your place of employment.

7. *Complete a personal inventory of your soft skills.* Now that you know what soft skills are and how important they are to your future, you are better equipped to identify them within your own life. You may have many of the skills already in place from your previous work and life experience. Take stock. Get them integrated and into your résumé and vebalized into your interview presentations with prospective employers.

8. *Seek out managerial and peer review and feedback.* How else are you going to grow in your soft skills without getting feedback from the people who know you the most? Find a mentor, a boss, or trusted colleague who can help give you feedback about the soft skills we listed in this chapter and how they are working or need improvement in your work style. Get an outsider's opinion. Don't completely rely on your own assessment of yourself.

9. *Volunteer your services at a nonprofit organization.* Organizations like the Red Cross, United Way, and Toys for Tots all need you and many others as well. Better yet, you need them to try out new skills that you normally would not have a chance to develop at your current place of employment. Volunteer organizations demand more in the way of creativity, initiative, and implementation. Volunteer and you'll come out the winner, too.

10. *Explore the arts.* What have the arts got to do with busi-

ness? Everything! To develop creativity on the job, develop creativity within. Take up gardening. Start piano lessons. Learn to paint. Attend foreign language classes. Activities such as these utilize areas of the brain that inspire creativity in all of us. Within a few months, you'll come to work with a new and fresh outlook on work assignments, innovation, creativity, and the ability to learn new things at your job.

The Hard Skills

"Even as many corporations are conducting expensive nationwide searches for qualified employees," states Jeff Joseph, executive vice president of education and training for the U.S. Chamber of Commerce, "thousands of job applicants are being turned away from corporate personnel departments because they lack the basic skills required to function in the workplace. By and large, these disappointed job seekers are individuals who, in an industrial era economy, would have been able to acquire and keep well-paying jobs in business and industry."

In the past, workers *maintained* the muscle of machinery and heavy industry to succeed. The future is here now, and it's different than the past. Workers now succeed by restructuring and reinventing their knowledge of technology and information transfer and access. We must be committed to transforming ourselves, our attitudes, and above all our skills.

Jeff Joseph spoke before a House committee about the future world of work and what he calls the "Age of Transformation." He addresses how we got here and where we as workers should be going with our skills if we are to succeed:

The world is immersed in a rare and unprecedented era of technological transformation that is rapidly remaking virtually every aspect of the way we work and live. The computer chip was an unprecedented breakthrough, greater in its implication than the internal combustion engine, the telephone and the radio. While the machines of the industrial age magnified the power of the human muscle, the computer chip magnifies the power of the human mind. The impact is awesome because intellect is the greatest power of all. The influence of the chip is growing exponentially. Twenty years ago there were only 50,000 primitive computers in existence and a like number of people who could handle them. Today, 50,000 computers are sold every ten hours, an explosive marketplace driven by a growing throng of eager enthusiasts constantly seeking out new applications for the extraordinary power placed at their disposal. In this rapid-paced high-tech modern workplace the workers must be highly literate and computer friendly and able to relearn their basic skills constantly.

The U.S. Chamber of Commerce surveyed the readers of their membership magazine, *Nation's Business*. They asked their members about their education and training needs. A full 93 percent reported that new employees lacked adequate job skills and preparation. A whopping 97 percent reported that skill levels had either declined or remained the same in the past five years.

In a similar study of 100 personnel managers done by the Cambridge Human Resource Group, a Chicago consulting outfit, more than 40 percent report that their firms' employees worry about what talents and abilities will be expected of them in the workplace of the future; by contrast, only 17 percent say employees fret about the stresses of their current jobs.

Are You Really Techno Literate or Techno Illiterate?

Are you ready for the future now? How ready are your hard skills for the challenge of the electronic workplace? Has technology become an integral part of your profession? Which has become the dinosaur, you or the PC that sits turned off or unused, decorating your desk? You be the judge. Take the techno literacy test.

Techno Literacy Test

(Circle "Y" for yes or "N" for no for each of the following statements)

Y   N   Do you have a computer you use regularly either at home, work or school?

Y   N   Have you used each of the following types of software programs: spreadsheet, word processing, Windows, and database applications?

Y   N   Do you feel comfortable using on-line technology, such as the Internet?

Y   N   Do you send and receive E-mail on a frequent basis?

Y   N   Have you subscribed to an on-line service?

Y   N   Do you think overall technology has been our friend and created more jobs than it has displaced?

Develop the Right Skills

Y	N	Have you taken any training classes within the past twenty-four months to boost your technological skills?
Y	N	Have you ever received or downloaded a file via modem?
Y	N	Could you locate a directory and its contents from a DOS prompt?
Y	N	Have you ever loaded new software onto a computer in a Windows environment?
Y	N	Have you ever gone on-line to do research for work, school, or personal use?
Y	N	Are you planning to take any training classes to boost your technological skills?
Y	N	Do you try to minimize paper usage and maintain most of your files, contacts, and schedules on a computer?
Y	N	Have you ever published a report in a professional format from your computer?
Y	N	Do you know how to import graphics into your reports?
Y	N	Have you gone on-line to chat with special interest groups?

Scoring: For every yes, give yourself 6 points. Add up your total score

6–30   You are a dinosaur! Quick, before you become extinct, it's never too late to save your species. Study the techno lingo table coming up next and implement the action steps listed below to improve your hard, technical skills.

36–60   So you're not a dinosaur, but don't become too elated. You are still on the endangered species list. You need to work to improve your skills by studying the techno lingo table and implementing the action steps listed below.

66–78   You are on the right track. With a bit more effort, you will be in total control of your future in the world of work. With a little more improvement, you will always remain quite marketable in the job market.

84–96   You have taken control of your skills, your life, and work. With your technical skills, you literally can create your own successes. You constantly remain curious and continuously seek to update your skills. Combined with a good image and attitude, you will never be out of a job for any extended period of time.

Techno Lingo

**Along with new skills, the professionals of the future must learn
a new language. Here is a glossary of terms you might need in order to
navigate through the outset of the twenty-first century.**

Term	Definition
BBS (Bulletin Board System)	An on-line system that allows special interest groups and other users to exchange messages and information
bps (bits per second)	A measure that indicates the speed at which data is transferred by a modem
Broadband network	A network that uses separate channels to transfer data, voice, and video at the same time
Chat	The ability to talk to other users in real time by typing messages
Cyberspace	The whole range of information resources available through computer networks
Domain	The name of an Internet service provider, which follows the @ symbol of an Internet address (Example: gjgjoseph@aol.com)

Develop the Right Skills

Term	Definition
E-mail (Electronic Mail)	A system of sending messages from one computer to another through a network or via on-line services and the Internet
FTP (file transfer protocol)	Allows Internet users to transfer files from one computer to another over phone lines or a network
Gateway	A computer that connects one computer to another, even though each may use different protocols
Gopher	A menu-based system that helps the user to search the Internet
Home page	An organization's site or presence on the World Wide Web
HTML (hypertext markup language)	The coding language that is used to create pages for the World Wide Web. It creates the display of fonts and graphics that you see on a page
HTTP (hypertext transfer protocol)	The system that allows World Wide Web pages to be transmitted over the Internet (Example: http://onstage.nyc.com/dialog.htm)
Hypertext	A method of writing and displaying text and graphics that allows a user to click on and and jump to related documents
Mailing list	Also called a listserv, an E-mail address that remails all incoming mail to subscribers interested in a given topic
Modem (*mo*dulator/*dem*odulator)	The device that allows a computer to connect to other computers via the phone lines

Term	Definition
Newsgroup	A BBS that allows users access to discussion on a given topic
Snail mail	Traditional mail services
TCP/IP (transmission control protocol/ Internet protocol)	The basic protocol that allows computers to communicate over the Internet
WWW (World Wide Web)	A sophisticated hypertext system that allows the user to browse the Internet, viewing text, graphics, video, and receiving sound

Sources: Matisse Enzer/Internet Literacy Consultants

Ten Action Steps to Improve Hard Skills

Here are ten action steps you can take to make sure you are entering the future world of work with training and experience in the necessary hard skills.

1. *No pay, no perks, no promotions, but volunteer.* You had read earlier about improving your soft skills by volunteering. It works the same for improving your hard skills. Give some of your time at a nonprofit organization and get involved in activities like generating computer-based mailing lists, data input, list merges, generating fund-rasing documents in word processing, financial record keeping, and Internet communications. These organizations are much more likely to give you the chance to try out or learn a new technical skill. After all, you don't cost anything, and whatever you accomplish is more than what they had. You both

come out winners. Remember, for all the learning and benefits you personally receive when you volunteer, free work is as serious as paid work.

2. *Use a friend.* It's generally not polite to use a friend, but in this instance it is. Find a friend or acquaintance at home or at the office who is techno literate. Develop a relationship where you can buddy up on his or her computer. Ask for a few minutes of his or her time occasionally to give you a few tips and insights. Here is a good formula for effective learning when you buddy up with a friend.

Cycle of Learning

1. They tell you why, how, and what they are going to do.
2. You observe while they do it.
3. You summarize and tell them why, how, and what they did.
4. You do it.
5. They give you feedback as to how to improve, and the cycle of learning begins again.

Of course, always recognize people who are willing to take time with you. Let them know they are appreciated. Often just a thank you note or a small gift is appropriate. I once took computer lessons from a friend, and in turn, I offered to help paint his house on a Saturday. It was a real deal for both of us.

3. *Play.* I've had some of my best breakthroughs at the computer by just having fun. No manuals, no books, no tutors, just trial and error. Set aside some time just to play. It may sound unproductive, but generally it is quite the opposite. Of course, don't try this technique on an important document. Be sure to

always maintain a copy of an important file before beginning any playtime. That is a major rule in the computer business: Maintain copies of anything important.

4. *Take the day off.* You can tell your boss you read it here. Take the day off! Of course, you are going to make it productive. Enroll in a one-day class in a particular area of computer technology or a software application that is currently needed to improve your skills. You will the find the right school by researching companies in the telephone directory under *computer training.* Ask for their client list and instructor qualifications before enrolling. Ask if the company will reimburse you for the cost of the one-day seminar. Don't be surprised if they won't. And don't be surprised if it has to be on your personal time. Sorry, but I want to prepare you for what could be reality in many instances. Still, don't be discouraged. Take the class anyway. Remember, it's all about building your skills and your résumé for the future.

5. *Read a good book.* A shocking statistic I read a few years ago was that only 20 percent of the American population reads one or more books a year. It's no wonder that for so many of us, our knowledge base and skills are lagging. You can be different from the rest. Pick up books on technology and computer software. Become an avid reader and introduce yourself to a whole new world of information and knowledge.

6. *Go back to school.* So far, most of the action steps have been relatively quick fixes. Going back to school is not. But sometimes drastic circumstances require drastic measures. Take, for instance, Florence, who lives in State College, Pennsylvania, home of Penn State University. In the latter part of her career, she took the effort to become completely educated in current technology. She is familiar with scanners, importing graphics, report formats,

desktop publishing, and more. As Florence has demonstrated, it's never too late to learn. If your skills are completely outdated, going back to school and taking a weekend or night class, no matter what age you are, may be the most appropriate and aggressive step you could take to make you and your career competitive well into the future. Charles Handy, the author of *The Age of Unreason*, summarizes the importance of learning in this age quite well. He states, "If changing is really learning, if effective organizations need more and more intelligent people, if careers are shorter and more changeable, above all, if more people need to be more self-sufficient for more of their lives, then education has to become the single most important investment that any person can make in their own destiny."

7. *Invest in the home.* For many, having computer technology at home may be considered frivolous or a luxury that one cannot afford. Update your thinking. A computer at home is *not* a luxury but a necessity. It will pay itself off in the long-term benefits of updating your work skills, educating your children, and managing your home and finances. Let's not forget the hours of fun and entertainment it will provide as well.

8. *Call for help.* Lost on the highway, we sometimes continue to drive without stopping to get directions. We soon discover that a simple stop to ask directions many miles back could have saved a lot of aggravation. Don't be proud. No matter how simple or difficult a computer task may be, take the time to call the software company's support number and get further information and clarification about your situation. Sometimes just call to learn something new about your computer's software that you may have not been able to learn by simply reading the manual.

9. *Ask questions.* Similar to the last point, don't hesitate to pick

up the phone or go to a colleague's desk to ask a question and get clarification to learn something new about a computer task. Many perceive asking questions of others as a sign of weakness. It is quite the opposite. Ask questions and you will learn incessantly and at a more rapid pace than those who don't. Never lose a childlike, inquisitive mind. It is the sure sign of a winner.

10. *Let a computer teach you.* The very thing that you may fear most actually has the ability to teach you. Most computer programs come with a resident tutorial. Take the time to work through the tutorials of the software programs you ought to know in order to update your skills. Log on to the tutorial and in a few short moments you and the computer will interact, coaching you to new heights.

Follow the action steps in this chapter, and you will arrive in the future competitive, updated, extremely marketable, financially secure over the long term, and unstoppable.

STRATEGY 4

Learn to Sell Yourself Like a Company Sells a Product

"Why do I need to learn to sell myself?" you may ask. In one word, *competition*. The trends that have reshaped the workplace of the future have made getting a job extremely competitive. For example, smaller companies with a half million dollars worth of high-tech equipment can run itself with only ten employees. Big corporations continue to downsize as management ranks are being thinned and dismantled. Even the front-line workers are being dismissed as computer-savvy coworkers and managers can now do the work of many from a single computer. One human resources executive compared getting a job in a tight market with qualifying for and competing in the Olympic Games. Few are chosen, even fewer bring home the gold.

Think of Yourself as a Product

Staying employed in the twenty-first century means using the latest sales and marketing techniques to get, keep, and be promoted in the job you want. People have to think of themselves as a product. Just as companies and stores sell products, so you have to learn to sell yourself. As a human resources executive for many years, it has been my experience that the people who get the best jobs are not necessarily the most qualified. It is actually the people who know how to market themselves most effectively. As a human resources professional, I am most inclined to not only rely on a résumé, but the total presentation such as communication, persuasion, and image to make a decision to hire. Most human resources professionals I speak with agree.

Like a corporation, you have a unique set of skills and assets (the sum total of your work and life experiences) that translated, are your "products and services" that you need to sell to others. However, most of us are not trained to think in terms of self-promotion. C. J. Polk, a manager of the materials engineering section for Mobil Oil, states, "I think this is particularly true in many engineering managers. We are trained to think in specific, no-nonsense terms. I, for example, am completely turned off by advertising hype and can be a real hard sell to a car salesperson. However, as engineering managers, we're currently being encouraged by our top management to market our technology to our clients so they can make the best use of our services. We have to learn how to do it effectively if we are to compete." Truxtun Gowen, a career consultant in the Northeast, agrees. "Whenever there is greater competition, people have to sell more effectively. Sales is a process of differentiation. You have to differentiate yourself in the workforce."

Negative Images of Selling

Throughout the country I've heard many of the participants in my career seminars proclaim, "If I wanted to sell, I would have gone into sales." To many, the mere idea of selling conjures up negative images of devious salespersons in plaid suits selling used cars that don't work. Selling for many has taken on the negative images of dishonesty, a shyster or hard-sell mentality. Some of us resist selling ourselves simply because of a false sense of humility, modesty, or shyness. As George Bush's mother said, "Don't brag!"

A marketing manager for a major hotel company in the Northeast found it difficult to promote himself when faced with a recent downsizing and termination. Daily he used his marketing skills to promote the unique qualities of his company's hotel as a business meeting destination. Yet, faced with promoting himself, he was unable to do it. He states, "I think it all comes from the way you were raised. I grew up in a home where we were deeply religious. My father taught us, 'To God be the glory.' It was inappropriate to toot your own horn, so to speak."

Selling "Me, Inc." Takes Work

The whole idea of selling yourself can sound like a lot of work. In fact, I am of the opinion that many try to excuse themselves from the hard work of learning how to sell. In the new world of work, winners can no longer excuse themselves from this enormous responsibility. Selling skills are a necessity. Keep in mind that self-marketing at its best and most subtle form is a skill to be admired. Selling yourself does not have to take on the aura of the used-car salesperson described above. But above all, it is work and it takes practice.

In chapter five of my book *Get the Job You Want in Thirty Days*, I review what I call the five steps to selling. It walks you through interview practice sessions and self-selling role-plays that I've set up for you. In another book, *The Top 10 Fears of Job Seekers*, I have a chapter that concerns itself with the fear of self-selling and how to overcome that fear and place it into proper perspective in your life. From my previous books here is an overview to the basics of self-selling that you should be aware of when promoting yourself.

Thirteen Tips to Selling Yourself

1. Get the interviewer to like you in the first thirty seconds.
2. Smile, use the interviewer's name, offer a sincere compliment or icebreaker.
3. Learn about the employer's needs.

4. Ask open-ended questions.
5. Assume at all times that you will get the job.
6. Discover what their main problems and concerns are.
7. Offer yourself as the solution.
8. Never state a fact or feature about yourself without stating a benefit to the employer.
9. Express enthusiastic and sincere interest in the job.
10. Ask for the job at the interview. Don't assume they think you want it.
11. Create urgency in the hiring process such as hinting that other offers are forthcoming.
12. Follow up.
13. Never give up.

Not addressed in my previous books are two additional self-marketing techniques that you need to know in order to effectively sell yourself.

Develop a Sight-Seller

The first technique is to develop what I call a sight-seller. Whether you are employed or unemployed, go out and buy a small black portfolio with approximately 8½" × 11" plastic protective sheets on the interior. Begin to make a scrapbook portfolio documenting your work projects and successes that you can share with future prospective employers at an interview. The scrapbook is very similar to the portfolios that salespeople carry and present on sales calls to prospective clients about their products and services.

To say what you have done is one thing; to show it and visually document it is highly effective and convincing to the listener. Here are just a few of the many visuals you could be collecting and inserting to build your sight-seller to be more convincing at your next self-selling situation:

- Letters of recognition from customers
- Letters of recognition from immediate managers and upper management
- Company awards
- Community service awards
- Product brochures you worked on, sold, or developed
- Task force documents that demonstrate your participation
- Published articles
- Work simplification ideas you implemented
- An outline of all projects you engaged in at your previous employer
- Photographs that document your work-related successes
- Current and past employers' marketing brochures
- Professional seminars' certificates of completion

Now that you have a few ideas of where to begin, take the initiative to be creative and start building your sight-seller. Once you have it initially put together, update it as frequently as necessary to reflect new accomplishments and achievements. You may even use it to present your case for an internal promotion or pay increase. It's a tool that will give you the cutting edge over the competition when selling "Me, Inc." Above all, it will help you remember all the things that you do that really make you valuable but sometimes are taken for granted and may have even been forgotten. Now that you know about building a sight-seller, once you do it, bring it to your next internal promotion presentation or external job interview. Don't leave home without it.

Develop an Action Plan

Recently I spoke with Kelly, who is preparing to move from Central Florida to the Miami/Fort Lauderdale area with his wife and newborn child. Upon completing his interview for the position of staff writer in a medium-sized company's marketing department, he was a bit concerned to hear that there were three other competitors vying for the same job. A one-in-four chance of getting the job was worrisome. To differentiate himself from the competition, Kelly set out to write and overnight air express an action plan for his first ninety days of employment. He sent it to the key decision maker along with copies to the others who interviewed him. This approach definitely puts Kelly in the forefront of the competition. It also gives him a good reason to call and follow up a few days later. When he calls, he simply asks his interviewer, "What did you think about my action plan?" He then proceeds with salesmanlike closing statements such as, "When will the hiring decision be made? When will I start?" Both questions are open-ended. They demand a more open response than a simple yes or no. The action plan creates a much better reason to call and follow up. Without it, the follow-up phone call would sound rather weak, such as, "Did I get the job?" This is a close-ended question and does not elicit a more open and possible positive response.

Pointers for Developing a Combination Follow-up Action Plan and Letter

- Thank them for the interview.
- Explain how your keen interest in the company and position prompted the creation of the following action plan.
- Base the plan first of all on what you will immediately do to manage the current business at hand.
- Secondly, discuss what you perceive to be the long-term problems and issues confronting the position and their corresponding solutions. Explain how you will manage the future and its challenges.
- Describe any product or work improvements you perceive at this early juncture. However, keep the comments positive and not insulting in any way. If you are in doubt, don't say it.
- Based on what you learned in the interviews and your research, address any other issues with action plans and ideas that may come to mind.
- End the letter with a close for the reader to take action, such as "When can we discuss this further? I can be reached at [and give your telephone number]."

The only risk you take in developing a ninety-day action plan—and for that matter it could even be a twelve month plan—is that you lack complete knowledge of their business. It is quite possible that your ideas may be rejected. The upside to this scenario is that, although your ideas were not totally on target, your creativity, assertiveness, ability to think, and ability to take action will be admired. There is no doubt about it. You've just set yourself apart from your competitors, whether they be internal or external. Of course, we never tell our competitors what marketing tactics we are using. Keep any unique strategies that you have developed a secret.

Self-Selling Checklist

In closing, here is a checklist to review and determine if you are adequately prepared to sell yourself. If you determine that you are weak in any area, you know what you should do: Fix it!

- Prepare a professional image. Your product packaging can make a difference.
- Maintain an organized and clean office. The way it looks influences others.
- Speak in a clear and audible manner.
- Utilize gestures when you speak. Be animated but not overly dramatic.
- Own at least two classic and conservative business outfits.
- Know at least five things about yourself that make you unique in the marketplace.
- Make at least one new contact a month and sell yourself whether you need a job or not.
- Return phone calls the same day (maximum twenty-four hours).
- Develop your own personal sight-seller.
- Have a current one-page teaser résumé for cold contacts.

- Have a current two-page extended résumé for warm contacts. (See *Get the Job You Want in 30 Days*. It explains how to do this.)
- Have a current cover letter that sells at least two facts or features about "product you" and the corresponding benefits to a company's goals and bottom line.
- Have a current business card on you at all times, even on vacation.
- Listen well.
- Smile. People who do have higher credibility.
- Smile when you are on the telephone.
- Ask open-ended questions well.
- Take notes.
- Remember to use people's names.

STRATEGY 5

Build a Network

Usually, when a person sends out a résumé, it is in a time of crisis and need. You know the scenario: Rumor has it that the impending corporate ax is looming, or it's Friday morning and the pink slips have just been given out. All of a sudden it is discovered that it's time to send out résumés and start networking. Wrong! Success in the future means aggressively and decidedly being determined to stay plugged in, no matter how good you think you currently have it. People will have to sow the seeds of effective networking well in advance of reaping the benefits.

After four grueling months of networking with literally thousands of contacts and landing a job at the helm of a Seattle start-up, what did Tom Borger do next? Even more networking. Borger sent out more than 1,000 thank you notes with cards announcing his new assignment. They went to friends, former colleagues, executive recruiters, and anyone else who took the time to offer advice and referrals. Tom Borger, like many who are suddenly laid off, found out what it's like to be out of touch and out of work. He states in the January 11, 1996, issue of *Investor's Business Daily*, "It was horrifying to realize how unconnected I was. Suddenly, you look around and say, 'How could I have let this happen?' "

Networking is an ongoing process. But how many of us really believe it and practice it? As we discussed in the previous chapter, you are responsible for marketing the company and product "Me, Inc." You and only you are responsible for marketing that product on a continuous basis.

Successful Networking

Successful networking takes consistency over time. It is not an easy thing to do when you are working hard at your current job. However, if you try to do it just when you need a job, people will instantly sense that. They feel like they are being used. Your efforts at this point become ineffective and counterproductive. The most successful networkers are those who believe that their professional life, community service, and personal life are one. Similar to a drop of color dye in water, they become inseperable.

Various studies have shown, depending on the one you read, that between 65 percent and 80 percent of all new jobs are found through networking. This statistic is congruent with the U.S. Department of Labor statistic that 80 percent of all jobs available are never published. They obviously are found only through networking.

Networking Strategies

In my experience, networking strategies are what most people lack. Clearly defined networking strategies are what it takes to propel a career forward into unlimited boundaries and success. Here are my top twenty-five networking strategies that should be consistently integrated into your daily and personal style. If you are currently using any of these strategies, keep up the good work. Make a commitment today to implement the ones that you are not currently using. By implementing them, you take control of the future. Don't let the uncertainties of the future control you. And, by the way, the scientific formula for networking is as predictable as mathematics. What you get out of it is in direct proportion to the amount of dedication and energy that you put into it.

Top Twenty-five Networking Strategies

1. *Develop ties with various key people in your company in other departments.* Call them occasionally, stop by their office, take a fifteen-minute coffee break together, or better yet, take them to lunch. Do this as frequently as possible. Besides increasing your personal visibility, you get plugged in and informed about important happenings that will help secure your career.

2. *Edit, write, or contribute articles to your company's news-letter.* It's a great way to learn more about the company, industry, and product. It also keeps your name in front of the rest in the

organization. You can even start your own departmental newsletter and become the self-appointed editor. Other departments will soon copy your success. It's a great way to become known as an innovator.

3. *Volunteer to be put on any major task forces or committees being formed within your company.* Of course, always go for the ones with the most visibility, scope, and organizational influence. You want the most recognition you can get in return for the time you have invested.

4. *Make presentations.* Whenever you have the opportunity to stand up in front of a department or companywide meeting to discuss an idea or project, take advantage of it. It's free advertising for "product you."

5. *Become a member of key trade organizations in your field of expertise.* Attend the local chapter's meetings. Network and pass out business cards at each meeting. Don't be shy. Make presentations and give speeches whenever possible.

6. *Get involved in key civic and nonprofit organizations.* You can maximize the return on this activity by becoming an active contributor to these types of organizations. Build solid relationships with key members. Don't be a passive member.

7. *Spend time with the winners in life.* Spend your business and personal free time with the movers and shakers of this world. Learn from them and let them mentor you. Don't be proud. Avoid spending much of your time with complainers and negative thinkers. They do not in any way have the ability to motivate you or connect you to future career success.

8. *Become a teacher.* Hook up with the human resources and training departments of your company. Teach a class in an area of expertise that will help other employees. You can also become

a teacher by taking a part-time position at a local university, college, or technical school.

9. *Publish articles and essays.* Write for professional and trade journals. Once your writing is published, make sure the influential people in your life get copies.

10. *Tell others that they're doing a good job.* Praise others and their accomplishments. Become their greatest fan. It's a sincere way to win people's trust and confidence. They become your fan as well.

11. *Notify the press of your accomplishments.* Make sure your local newspaper and trade journals are aware of your successes and achievements. This is no time to be shy. Get your name out there and take advantage of the free publicity.

12. *Listen a lot.* By some this is called the art of small talk. It is literally what it says: Listen a lot and talk a little.

13. *Use people's names.* Refer to people by name the moment you first meet them. A good habit to get into in order to remember names is to use a new person's name at least twice within the first ten seconds of meeting him or her.

14. *Be the first to introduce yourself.* Walk into a room of new people and be the first to extend your hand, greet, and meet someone new. Don't wait for others to make the first approach. Most won't. You will connect with more people faster with this assertive style.

15. *Have a firm handshake.* Also, smile and maintain eye contact when shaking another person's hand.

16. *Get comfortable with using icebreakers.* An icebreaker has *nothing* to do with business. "How's your day going today?" is not an icebreaker. "What do you think about this weather we've been having lately?" is an icebreaker. Use icebreakers to meet

new people and engage them in neutral conversation. Once you both feel comfortable, it will lead to productive networking and business discussions.

17. *Target your market and conversation*. When networking with others, discuss examples from your life and work history that have the most relevance to their needs and situation.

18. *Take notes*. You appear responsible, trustworthy, and frankly, you remember more. Carry a small notepad in your pocket or write on a business card if you are in a pinch.

19. *Develop relationships*. Don't expect instant results from your efforts. Nurture your new friendships and relationships over time.

20. *Don't prejudge people*. It may be that person you neglected to talk to because of a bad first impression that actually has the ability to hire you or connect you to the right person.

21. *Make others feel important*. Ask good open-ended questions about their career, successes, hobbies, and interests. Be sincerely interested in the other person.

22. *Value other people's time*. Always ask, "Is this a good time to talk?" Or say, "Do you have a few moments to talk now or should I call later?"

23. *Help others get what they want*. Networking works both ways. When the phone rings or someone comes to your office and asks for help, be prepared to do what you can to help the other person.

24. *Follow up*. Stay in touch with your contacts. Send them a thank you note for their assistance. However, beyond that, remember their birthday. You can make a phone call and just say hi for a moment. Buy them a small token gift that may represent a unique hobby or interest they may have; mail or give it to them.

Clip an article out of a magazine that suits their interests and make a special effort to give it to them.

25. *Maintain a database of contacts.* Implement a computerized system that tracks a contact's pertinent information such as name, address, work number, home number, family members, hobbies, interests, dates of special occasions, and gifts last sent. Once computerized, this list has the ability to notify you of monthly birthdays and special occasions as well as create your holiday card list and even address the envelopes.

On-line Networking Can Mean a Job Will Find You

The increasingly global market makes it impossible for you to be everywhere at once. To network effectively in the future, you also literally have to get plugged in—plugged in to the Internet that is. The ambitious professional should list his or her résumé on the Internet by subscribing to a number of on-line résumé banks. When your resume resides in an on-line database, it can be read instantly by companies and recruiters worldwide. An on-line résumé does the work for you. When a company does a search and they need your talents, your name will appear according to their search criteria and you will get a phone call. It's a simple yet massive and effective form of networking.

One company in particular that is well known for this service is the Technology Registry. They are the nation's largest and most sophisticated on-line employment database, according to *PR Newswire* (June 13, 1995). For Internet users, the Technology

Registry offers a free Fast Form to place a career snapshot into their database.

Another company, CareerMosaic, claims to be the premier career Web server on the Internet today. Hundreds of top employers have listed detailed profiles and exciting job opportunities from 3Com to Xerox. Their exclusive page, J.O.B.S. (Jobs Offered By Search) is currently used 50,000 times every day by applicants in the job market. The service maintains current information by updating and adding over 23,000 postings daily. CareerMosaic also features the Online Job Fair, attracting thousands of candidates from across the country. CareerMosaic can be checked out at www.careermosaic.com.

Some words of caution, Internet networkers beware: If you are currently employed, be sure your on-line résumé doesn't get downloaded by your current employer. You don't want it to end up in the wrong hands. One suggestion is to cross job markets with your electronic résumé. Redirect your talents and qualifications to a new industry. This technique will make it unlikely that your current employer would find you in any search, as theirs will probably be contained within your current industry.

To adequately round out your future networking techniques, combine the high-tech, Internet approach with the high-touch, down-to-earth, face-to-face approach discussed earlier. With all bases covered, you are plugged in, turned on, and always ready with a new career in waiting no matter what life circumstances come your way.

STRATEGY 6

Change Jobs Frequently

Change is scary. For most, routine is to be venerated and *change* is despised. If you don't believe it, when was the last time you changed your morning routine? Try it sometime and see how awkward change really feels. Try brushing your teeth first if you normally do it last, or style your hair last if you normally do it first upon exiting the shower. A simple exercise like this reinforces the fact that we are creatures of habit.

Making a successful living in the future lean and competitive world of work means changing jobs frequently, either internally or externally. It means becoming versatile, diverse, and knowledgeable in a wide area of skills and topics. The more diverse work experiences that you have, the more marketable you become. The more marketable you become, the less reliant you are upon your current employer for job fulfillment and financial security. By changing jobs frequently, you remain on the offensive and not the defensive side of driving your career to the goal line. It is an advantageous position to be in if you wish to remain in control of your future.

But isn't job hopping considered a sign of instability? Yes and no. Yes if the last five jobs you have had are in a span of six months, but not if the job changes you have embarked on have had even one to three year spans of employment, you left on good terms, and for good reasons other than that you disliked your boss. Job changing today is generally looked upon as more of a positive than a negative. In the past, it was a negative. Companies now see job changers as drivers, innovators who bring a wealth of knowledge and diverse experiences to the table that their own long-term workers are unable to provide.

Career Bridging

Now that you're convinced that self-inflicted job changing is in your best interest, welcome to the world of career bridging. "It has become an important futuristic career skill; the ability to make job changes in a time of corporate downsizings, reorganizations and little job security," reports Patricia Kitchen in the April 17, 1994, issue of *Newsday*.

How is Arnold moving from managing Manhattan co-ops to running elderly care facilities?

How is Susan, a television producer, positioning herself to ride the wave of interactive technology in her industry?

How is Carl engineering a transition from bank fraud investigations to public school administrator?

The answer to each is by taking one small, decisive step at a time. They know that moving into a new area does not happen overnight; it's a process.

Anna, a human resources professional for a major European international airline, is based in midtown Manhattan. Her job has been threatened for years as a result of new laws governing European airline deregulation resulting in increased competition and a possible merger. Overwhelmed by the thought of being laid off and changing jobs, she has done little to career bridge and make the necessary small steps to take control of her future. Letitia A. Chamberlain, director of the Center for Career and Life Planning at New York University responds, "They don't want to start all over, so often they stay right where they are."

Some people make the fatal error of thinking in terms of one dramatic jump, but it's the total opposite. It requires vigilance and commitment. In order to be an effective job changer you have to keep up with what's going on in your industry and other industries. It takes work and lots of it. You have to stay connected as we discussed in the previous chapter and above all develop flexible job skills and a variety of diverse work experiences.

Homos Jobus Hoppus

Younger workers are more inclined to take risks and change jobs frequently, according to Midwest Data Resources, Inc. A U.S. Department of Labor study shows that the typical working person holds 7.5 jobs by the age of thirty. After age thirty, they become less exploratory, more settled, and less likely to change jobs as frequently.

To remain competitive in the new economy, think about reviving your youthful zest for life and risk. Here are three steps that you should review and implement to be a successful Homos Jobus Hoppus. They are very simple: research, discuss, and act.

Research

Force yourself out of the everyday rituals you engage in while currently employed. It's easy to get into a rut. Through daily, weekly, and monthly research, get a picture of your own industry *and* an industry or two you would like to move into.

Research acts as sort of a reality check. After research, you may discover that what sounds like a hot future industry or job to you now is not worth pursuing, and your time would be better spent somewhere else.

Research is really the key to job hopping. Read business and trend articles in newspapers, professional magazines, and newsletters. You can even ask professional trade associations to send you one year of back issues of their newsletter. Skim the headlines for tips and helpful career guidance information. Expand your research by light years by subscribing to one of a number on-line research databases. One in particular, Lexis-Nexis, offers the ability to instantly research all current news on a particular topic by simply constructing a search string of words that describe the area you wish to research. Here you can access from one to hundreds of articles that give you the latest information on your industry of choice.

The goal of your research is both to become informed and to learn the problems, organization, key players, and jargon of the industry and job you wish to move into. You want to sound like an insider.

Discuss

This is a continuation of the research stage. The only difference is that you are now discovering information about your current or potentially new industry by talking with others. You are not out asking for a job, so please don't confuse this step with that activity. This is simply a discovery stage. It's just that now you sound more intelligent, plugged in, and asking the right questions based on the knowledge you have acquired in the first step.

Don't just meet people; have a goal. For instance, you may attend a local or regional trade association meeting or even a national convention in your industry. It's a great place to collect business cards, but go beyond that. Get answers to specific questions that will help drive your future. Ask questions such as: What are the top ten growth companies in this field in the country today? What are the best certification programs? How is this new growth industry being structured? You can think of many more.

Don't just talk to people who are in a position to hire you. There are many people you can speak with who can fill in the gaps in your knowledge base. Don't overlook the quiet person you may be riding in the elevator with every day. He or she could be an incredible visionary. Look for people, no matter what their status, who are charged, informed, and not satisfied with the status quo.

Act

Once you've engaged yourself long and hard enough in the above steps, you're ready to push yourself toward a target. Set your sights internally on a new position with your current employer or externally with another company. Begin the application process. Initiate phone calls, cover letters, and send out résumés. Before you start doubting, begin to move on to the next action without looking back. You know what happens when you look away from your goal in any sport? You lose the game.

In Summary

In order to promote oneself, engaging in self-inflicted job dislocation is a necessity in the future world of work. The workers who get ahead are not those with better skills but those who have the ability to make changes.

STRATEGY 7

Act as an Independent Contractor

Often at my career seminars I'll take a show of hands by asking the question, "How many here are self-employed?" Out of a large crowd, only one or two will raise their hands. Then I announce that it is actually a trick question because the answer is that we are *all* self-employed, whether we work for an employer or ourselves. To a majority of disbelievers, I explain how each of us actually works for oneself first and the company second. We all work first and foremost for "Me, Inc."

It has been my experience that many workers disagree with this valuable career insight. Many in my experience hold what I call a "1900s factory worker" mentality. That is, arrive to work on time, take a fifteen-minute morning and afternoon break, do only what is required of you, and go home when the clock says it's time to leave. One gentleman I hired for a company a few years ago epitomizes this mentality. Tom was recruited for the position of telemarketer for a small company in Miami, Florida. He was an educated and bright young man with a degree in business from the University of Michigan. However, his work ethic, the factory worker mentality, was his worst enemy for his own career and personal advancement. I knew we were in trouble when not long after his hire he began to question the longer work hours to accommodate our California customers. He also began to question the additional compensation for his travel days to visit clients in other cities. His rigid attitude of work, effort, and corresponding compensation demands was his demise. One of the partners in the firm eventually asked him to leave.

Tom was paid a competitive salary, commissions, and benefits. I recall speaking with him on a few occasions, asking him to lighten up and give the position his 200 percent. I concluded, "You are the one who will benefit." He continued to stick to his belief that he had to be compensated for anything he got involved in beyond the normal job description. He wanted a tight and well-defined role and work hours within the company and wanted to know exactly what he would get paid for that role. Instead of opting for personal growth, developing his résumé and experience from a diverse job description, he chose the status quo. He acted employed, as a typical worker. To act as an independent contractor and self-employed person, he would have had to deliver whatever he could to grow, expand his company, and reap long-term benefits for his business—a great mind-set that any successful small business owner should have.

In my opinion, too often workers opt for short-term gain for long, long-term loss. The benefit to the factory mentality in the short term is the little effort put out for an average wage. In the long term, the downside is that twenty years later the worker is still earning an average wage at the same position in a boring career. Because no one wants to take personal responsibility for this gross error in life, they blame others, the company, and bosses for their stagnation, frustration, and anger.

Five Steps to Becoming an Independent Contractor

Let's take a look at five steps to changing your internal attitude, if you haven't done so already, from a "1900s factory worker" mentality to one of "independent contractor."

1. *Make an internal decision to excel.* The starting point to "running your own business" and becoming an internal independent contractor begins here. If you are not ready or able to make a commitment to the pursuit of excellence, your career is in jeopardy. But how do we make that crossover and make the internal decision to excel?

For me, it was by observing others. When I worked at People Express Airlines, I remember looking around each day I came to work and seeing many individuals with more ambition and more commitment to excellence than me. I got jump-started by watching others. They inspired me to achieve and do better. I learned to excel from the people I admired the most who worked around me.

The other way I made the crossover to excel was by observing the reward, recognition, advancement, and promotions that the peak performers around me were enjoying. Some I observed were promoted internally. Others, I observed as they exited the company and, with their enthusiasm and experience, got better jobs somewhere else. Their gain inspired me to excel and become a peak performer, too.

Truxtun Gowen, a career consultant in the Northeast, is aware of interesting research done along these lines that he shares in his workshops. He states, "There was a recent study done where they had people come in to put together a puzzle. The ones who were paid stopped when the timer said stop. The ones who were not paid continued to work." The people who were not paid continued to contribute. The people who were being paid stopped working because they were being paid for the activity. The moral, he states, is "contributing has inherent benefits for the individual. It does more for the person than anyone else."

So, peak performers, those who contribute and commit to excel, in the final analysis believe that *they* come out the winner as a result of *their* efforts. They do not focus on what they might be losing, if they are being taken advantage of, or what they are not being paid for. Those who excel believe that they personally benefit from their efforts. A single theme exists in all of them, "I have done well, I am capable of achieving more, and I will always succeed."

2. *Act the part.* Commenting on success, the great German poet and writer, Goethe, said, "Before you can do something, you must first be something." In other words, before you can do what you would most like to do, you must first become the person who could do it. Yes, you must first act the part.

If your goal is to run a successful independent contracting business within your company, you must first act the part. If you want to excel and get to the next level, advance, and get promoted, you must begin now by acting the part. That means thinking, acting, and talking like company and department issues are yours. You need to *act* like an owner.

There is a story about Arnold Palmer, one of the great golf champions. When he was ten years old, he used to pretend that he was playing in national tournaments. He went as far as pretending to be a sports commentator announcing, "The champion, Arnold Palmer, is now ready to tee off." The moral of the story is, you can get very far in the game of work by acting as though you are playing in a great tournament.

By creating a mental image of being an owner, a supervisor, or manager of your company, you'll automatically begin to swing like the pros. By creating a mental image of the person you would like to become, by emulating him or her in everything you do, sooner or later you'll become that person. Doubt it? Give it a shot for thirty days and see what happens. *Act* the part. You've got nothing to lose.

3. *Don't let others block your career*. Being an independent contractor at your place of employment means owning and running your own internal business. As with any good business owner, don't let anyone else run the business for you. You are in charge.

Carol, for instance, was denied advancement from a secretary into a sales position by a boss who admitted the real reason he would not promote her was that "a good secretary is a lot harder to find than a good salesman." Possibly you have experienced a similar situation in your career. Sometimes individuals who don't take control of their business can get held back for all the wrong reasons.

Carol took control, realizing she was being held back. "I started job hunting and two months later, I found a job leasing earth-moving equipment to construction sites for a company twice the size of the one I was at, and for twice the money I had been earning as a secretary." Her former boss was shocked when she gave her notice. Two years later, Carol was promoted to the head of the leasing department. A year later, she took another job with a better company and is a manger in charge of a team of seventeen people in a sales department. "I make good money now," she said. "My only regret is that I wasted so much time accepting one person's view of how high I could reach in my career and forgot that one person did not have my best interest in mind."

If any person or persons is keeping your career paralyzed, you have no one to blame but yourself. No one is holding a gun to your head saying, "If you leave or make any changes in your life, I'm going to kill you." With that in mind, it's time to take charge of your business and take back the control you deserve, just as Carol did. You can do it, too.

4. *Be your greatest fan; promote yourself.* Know what your strengths are as an independent contractor and document them. Maintain a hero file for promoting your business. You know, the times when someone writes you a memo that says, "Gary, great job on the project." It's on letterhead, from the president or your boss. It goes directly to your hero file. Now you've got something substantial to bring with you in internal or external job interviews to promote yourself.

Another twist on the hero file is to change the usual to-do list into a running this-is-what-I've-done list. Keep the list updated weekly and track it in a computer's word processing software file.

Another way to promote your internal business is, at the end of every week, write a quick memo to your boss and copy your file. Tell the boss, exactly as an independent consultant would, what you have accomplished on company time that week. One person, Anne, got three promotions with this self-marketing technique in a period of a year and a half. Most people would have barely gotten one promotion in that same time period. It could be said that Anne knows how to run her independent contracting business very well, based on these kinds of results.

5. *Be loyal.* In the case of Anne, as discussed above, many people with long years of service often grumble when someone like her gets promoted. Although she did not have the long years of service that they had, she was loyal and deserving of advancement. One could argue that conventional wisdom has it that only individuals with a long term of service are loyal and should get promoted. They confuse their type of loyalty with Anne's. The only reason they are "loyal" in long years of service in the first place is probably because they do not have any market value on the outside.

Loyalty does not mean years. Further, people that grumble and talk are not loyal. To grow your internal business as an independent contractor means being loyal in a different sense. Loyalty means wherever you work, irrespective of years, there must be full dedication and devotion to the company. When you think about being internally self-employed, remember that being loyal to your "client" pays off, literally.

STRATEGY 8

Think National

The only limits we have in life are those that we place upon ourselves. One of the limits we often place on ourselves is the geographical location in which we have determined we will live and work. However, to be successful in the new economy requires mobility and flexibility on the part of career-minded individuals and their families. Thinking national and going national with one's career opens windows and worlds of opportunity that may no longer exist where we currently live. Here is one person's testimony of how he and his family broke out of old patterns of living in their comfort zone to achieve career and financial security.

"For almost a year my dream and that of my family's was to move from Los Angeles to New York to make a change for more growth in my career," says Jeff, formerly a press deputy for a Los Angeles city councilwoman. After much planning, taking initiative, and hard work, he has become successfully employed as press secretary for a New York City councilman. "A change to New York would have offered a broader political climate and opportunities for me to grow in my career. After three months of little free time and much determination, our dream has come true. In hindsight, I have no regrets of putting in the long hours of work and the financial risk that went along with fulfilling my dream."

Those who don't share Jeff's determination and drive may not understand people like him. Possibly they can't identify with that inner push for success. However, the dream of growing one's career, left unfulfilled, can result in resentment, financial difficulties, depression, general dissatisfaction, and a sense of defeat.

Similar to cross-country skiing, going national with your career and cross-country job hunting can be difficult at times and test your endurance. With a little bit of training, you can be prepared to win. Here are seven steps you can take to realize your dream:

- List the professional advantages and drawbacks.
- List the personal benefits and disadvantages.
- Communicate and gather feedback.
- Place key fears and barriers in perspective.
- Research the market.
- Write a plan.
- Implement the plan.

List the Professional Advantages and Drawbacks

Before embarking on a major move, be sure you are doing it for the right reasons. This requires some healthy introspection. Honesty is crucial. Ask yourself the question, What advantages will I gain in my career by thinking national and embarking on a cross-country move that I could not gain otherwise where I currently live? Make a list. Further, ask yourself, What are the potential disadvantages? Make a list. Take a moment and complete the following exercise.

Career Advantages and Disadvantages Exercise

Thinking National

Career Advantages	Career Disadvantages

The answers to these questions were clear for Carol, who is the former director of human resources at The Four Seasons Group. She is now director of human resources for The Scanticon International's Hotel and Conference Center at Penn State University. She states, "The advantage to me was to have something on my résumé that I would not have gotten where I was. By coming to Penn State Scanticon I had the opportunity to open a new hotel property. Opening a new property is an important key in the industry I work in." Carol explained that the disadvantages were going from a larger operation to a smaller one in size and business volume. However, Carol felt that what she gained far out-weighed any of the perceived drawbacks.

List the Personal Benefits and Disadvantages

Obviously, your whole decision is not going to be based strictly on career and professional reasons. Consider the personal benefits and disadvantages before going national with your career and embarking on a cross-country job hunt. After all, once you land your job, you're going to not only to have to work but balance leisure, sports, and other lifestyle activities. How will you feel about living there? List the *personal* benefits and disadvantages.

Personal Benefits and Disadvantages Exercise

Thinking National

Personal Benefits	Personal Disadvantages

William Frank, Jr., is president of The Curtiss Group. Since 1980, his firm has specialized in executive outplacement and is a member of Out Placement International. With many years of ex-

perience helping others go national with their careers and in helping with cross-country job hunts, he has discovered that the main
reasons behind this sort of transfer are often personal. "We get
calls all the time from people who want to move from one geographical location to another for personal reasons. For instance,
we have people who just don't like cold weather. If you are freez-
ing in Buffalo, Pittsburgh, or Detroit, then a cross-country job
hunt to the Sunbelt seems perfectly logical, regardless of the professional reasons."

Communicate and Gather Feedback

Going national with your career, moving to another city, and traveling across country is not a sudden event. In fact, after you have
clearly determined that the professional and personal advantages
and benefits outweigh the disadvantages, your initial work is still
not complete. Next, communicate with your spouse, key family
members, and friends. Ask for their feedback and opinions. By
no means should others be relied upon to make your life decisions, but gathering input is essential. And in the case of a spouse
or significant other, getting their support and agreement is critical.

For Jeff and his wife, negotiating a cross-country job hunt was
a gradual process of months of communication before making
the final decision to move. Jeff states, "It was one of the biggest
changes in our lives we would ever make. We discussed it a lot
and researched it. We called many friends and personal contacts
on both coasts and gathered as much information as we could."

With open communication at all levels, you are assured that

you have looked at all of the issues, that you have gained the support of key family members, and are prepared to work smart when the time comes to embark on the job hunt. It's a simple step, but one that could be costly if overlooked.

Place Key Fears and Barriers in Perspective

It is a normal reaction to have fears, worries, and concerns about the potential barriers one will have to overcome when doing something that one has never tried before. The important thing to realize is that in order to acquire your dream, each fear must be placed into proper perspective.

Generally, what do people worry about in a cross-country job hunt and move? William Frank, Jr., from The Curtiss Group, states, "Compensation is the main issue. Will I be paid the same? The next concern is how to conduct the search and arrange interviews over a long distance. Further, people have their concerns about schools, cost of housing, crime, and the cultural makeup of the community. Peripheral issues are also important such as shopping, sports, climate, and natural disasters."

One way to place your fears and concerns into proper perspective is to look at the whole process as an adventure and an opportunity, not as a win-lose situation. Look at it strictly as a win-win situation. In the short term, agree that you will take from the experience and the new job over the next year what you can to grow your résumé and career. In the long term, if it works, great! If it does not, you will move on to something else with more experience and with a broader outlook on life and your career.

Research the Market

Get a flavor for the community you wish to work and live in. Gain valuable information about career and lifestyle opportunities that may or may not meet your expectations. Before you move is the time to find out about these diverse issues. You don't want any major surprises once you have moved. How can you accomplish effective research about an area hundreds or thousands of miles away?

Carol, before moving to Penn State, was concerned about salary negotiations and researched wage and compensation benefits in her target city. "At the library, I looked in the B.L.R., *The Business and Legal Reports*, which publishes a compensation study and survey for each area of the country. When negotiation time came along, I knew exactly what that area paid. It also caused my potential employer to do their own research."

You can further your research by subscribing to the Sunday and Business Monday editions of the community newspapers in which you wish to live. A three-month subscription usually runs between fifty and sixty dollars. Also, the Chamber of Commerce is willing to send you all sorts of information about living in the new area including housing costs, businesses, schools, cultural activities, state and local tax structure, and more. The main branch of your city's library maintains copies of most cities' Yellow Pages. Here, you can get a handle on executive recruiters to fire off your résumé to, as well as potential employers.

Top Geographical Employment Growth Regions

To assist you in your career planning to think and act nationally, the following tables represent the top geographical growth regions of the United States going into the year 2000 and beyond. Use these tables to get your thought processes going and to enable you to strategize a national career move. You can keep this list current, update it, and modify it by remaining informed. Read publications like *The Wall Street Journal, Money, US News and World Report, Fortune*, and others.

The following tables present regional and state employment growth projections to 2005. It was compiled by the U.S. Department of Commerce, Survey of Business Trends. About every five years, these statistics are prepared to create a consistent set of detailed geographical projections within a national framework. Projections are prepared for states, regions, metropolitan areas, and economic areas. "These projections," states the U.S. Department of Commerce, "are based on the assumption that past economic relationships will continue and that there will be no major policy changes. The projections are neither goals for, nor limits on, future economic (or employment) activity in any geographical area."

Above-Average Growth by Region

A growth rate is projected to be *above* the U.S. growth rate of 1.5 percent per year in four Southern and Western regions. They are:

- Rocky Mountain
- Far West
- Southwest
- Southeast

Source: U.S. Department of Commerce

Below-Average Growth by Region

A growth rate is projected to be *below* the U.S. growth rate of 1.5 percent per year in four Northern and Central regions. They are:

- New England
- Plains
- Great Lakes
- Midwest

Source: U.S. Department of Commerce

In 1970, the Northeast and North Central regions contained more than half the country's population, 53 percent of the jobs, and 55 percent of personal income. By 1980, these regions had dropped to under half and continue on a decline destined to continue into the year 2000.

In summary, experts predict that the South and the West will account for two-thirds of the growth in jobs and more than half of the country's rise in income going into the year 2000 and beyond.

Write a Plan

Once you've conducted your research, the next step is to have a plan. After all, going for the gold in any sport, even if it is going national with your career and cross-country job hunting, doesn't happen by luck. You need a plan.

You'll want to write into your plan the following strategies:

- Get a local friend's or family's address to use.
- Have business cards and letterhead made up with the local address.
- Establish a local phone number with a voice mail service.
- Network the new city by phone. Call businesses and friends for referrals.
- Batch process your interviews and fly into town every few weeks.
- Solicit your church congregation and professional affiliations in the new city for referrals and support during the process.
- Write an approximate budget for the process. It's tax deductible.

Beyond the above-stated points, your plan should include strategies for returning phone calls from work if you are currently employed, i.e., using the pay phone in the building next door on your lunch hour. It should also include maximum use of your free time (little or no time for TV shows, on-line chat, and leisure activities) to generate cover letters, résumés, mailings, and follow-up.

Implement Your Plan

Plan your work and work your plan. Now you just have to do it. Remember your goal is not to get a job. That's right, it is *not* to get a job. It is first and foremost to accomplish that day's requirements of your game plan. A job offer in a new city is simply the *result* of a well-implemented plan.

So keep focused on your daily activities. Brian Tracy, author of the audio series, *The Psychology of Success*, states, "No matter how smart you are, if you *act* stupidly, then you are stupid. Being successful has nothing to do with intelligence. If you *act* intelligently, then you are intelligent." If you wish to realize your dream, all you have to do is *act* intelligently. That means *take action*!

STRATEGY 9

Go Global

With more companies going global, so is the future world of work. Especially for U.S. companies, by the late 1990s, more than 100,000 firms were engaged in some type of global venture, with a combined value of more than one trillion dollars. U.S. multinational companies employ almost seven million people outside the United States. For example, Colgate-Palmolive operates in 194 countries and receives approximately 70 percent of its eight billion dollars in annual revenues from overseas markets. AT&T has 52,000 employees working overseas in 105 countries. Bechtel Corporation has more than 30,000 employees in more than 70 countries. U.S. multinational companies like the ones just described, employ almost eighteen million people; that is almost 20 percent of the total U.S. employment. One out of every five workers works for a company with a global expanse.

But going global is not just for U.S. based companies. Foreign companies are also setting up operations in the United States. By the late 1990s, foreign multinationals account for the employment of over three million Americans and the figure is growing almost daily. Worldwide, foreign multinational companies account for the employment of seventy-three million people. The United Nations Conference on Trade and Development states that at the end of 1993 alone, the foreign multinational companies had accumulated assets worth over two trillion dollars.

In short, growth for companies and their workers of the future know no borders. Foreign assignments are becoming more and more a possibility for many workers who wish to advance their careers. For instance, Julie, a planning analyst for Honeywell, had considered an assignment overseas frequently. However, she kept dismissing it. It would be a lot to ask of her husband Mark, who would have to quit his accounting job. After further family discussions and even some with globe-trotting friends, she decided to go for it. Now they are back after eighteen months in Brussels with better jobs and few regrets.

As companies go increasingly global, international assignments are becoming a great way to advance a career and are a critical stepping-stone to becoming highly marketable in the new world economy. Medtronics, a medical devices company, has sent about forty of its employees overseas in recent years. "We want future leaders of the company to have a more global perspective," states Mary Ann Donahue, Medtronic's vice president, human development, in the November 5, 1995, issue of the *Star Tribune*. "It is becoming more and more a prerequisite."

Small- and Medium-Sized Companies Offer the Most Potential

International careers for Americans are far different in the future world of work than they were even a decade ago. Opportunities are no longer confined to large conglomerates with a branch office in every major city. The greatest growth in U.S. companies abroad is in small- and medium-sized firms. According to a quote from the September 11, 1995, issue of the *Los Angeles Times*, "When we're talking about where there are opportunities, I don't think we're seeing a large explosion of Americans placed abroad among large companies," says J. Michael Geringer, an international management consultant and business professor at Cal Poly in San Luis Obispo. "But I've certainly seen a lot of jobs open up in small and medium-sized enterprises. They seem to be benefiting an enormous amount from export opportunities the cheaper dollar provides."

There Are a Number of Factors to Consider

In order to take your career global and enjoy its long-term benefits, there are a number of factors to consider before you take the next flight out. Here are some of the issues you will want to think about, and you should prepare a game plan to address them.

The Right Match

Many consultants and human resources professionals agree that one of the trickiest challenges that will confront you in embarking on a global career is matching the right opportunity with your personality type and professional goals. For example, if you are a big city person, relocating to Jakarta may cause real problems. Most people feel they would like to relocate *anywhere* until the actual remote places and opportunities begin to be discussed.

The Family

Often, family is another big consideration. For instance, there is always the dual career dilemma. How does the nontransferred spouse find work in a foreign country? Often, the trailing spouse can get a job within the same company, but some companies have nepotism policies preventing this sort of hire.

One way to get around this issue is for the spouse to consider using the time for other opportunities that may help further his or her career. He or she may get involved in writing a book, doing volunteer work, or learning a foreign language. After all, foreign assignments usually come with excellent pay and many perks that will make up for the lost second family income.

Workers with teenage children also present a dilemma when considering an international transfer. You may want to discuss this sort of move with the children as they may be reluctant to interrupt their high school years, especially if you would be moving to an area where educational opportunities could be limited.

Training

To the degree that you train and prepare for an overseas assignment, you will help ease the transition there and make it a successful experience. Training should focus first of all on language.

It's best to prepare now for a potential career abroad by taking a foreign language in your spare time. The best way to accomplish this is to hire a private tutor to come to your home or to attend organized classes in your community. I have always had the best results with a private tutor. I like the advantage of learning at an accelerated rate as opposed to the classroom where others can hold me back. Also, the tutor has provided me with flexible learning time to fit my schedule. This is important when you have a busy career to manage. A tutor can also focus in on your business and related vocabulary. The next best way to augment your foreign language lessons is to make visits to the country whose language you are learning to speak. Don't stay in hotels, however. Stay in pensions and small guest inns where you have the opportunity to mix with the locals and English is rarely spoken.

Other training should focus on cultural nuances that could be critical in business and day-to-day survival. I like to call it cultural literacy. Learn about customs that are most appropriate in the foreign culture but are not learned or utilized here in America. For instance, in France it is considered offensive to address a senior citizen or elder in the familiar tense of a verb. It may even be considered offensive to address your boss and superiors in the familiar tense as well. Handshaking and eye contact are also American cultural practices that do not always translate well, especially in Far East countries. Learn what it takes to fit in. Learn about how they dress and gradually build a wardrobe that you feel comfortable in, yet allows you the ability to visually fit their environment. Learning about a country's culinary customs, dinning, and table manners is always an important issue and one that even your children will need to be trained in if traveling with them abroad. One mistake to avoid: Do not project American culture and customs on your new host country. Avoid phrases like, "In the U.S. we do it this way." Go with an attitude to experience the country and culture for what it is. Don't try to export American-ism when you take leave for your new assignment abroad. Just be prepared to export your technical and job knowledge. That is what the country and company will benefit from the most. For the best and most enriching experience, be prepared to immerse yourself in the country's culture. This, of course, depends on your family's interests and the degree of difference between the two cultures.

Prepare for Culture Shock

Coming back, the culture shock may actually be worse than go-ing. Many times, returning home can be a real letdown. I remem-ber after an extended assignment abroad in France, upon returning to the United States, I had an initial sense of not fitting in. It was difficult relating to American daily lifestyles and rituals after I had acquired so many new ones in France, all to be given up in just a twelve-hour flight from Paris. Another major factor was my noticeable lack of knowledge about American pop cul-ture—politics, events, and entertainment, which had occurred in the time I was away. I was often at a disadvantage in conversa-tions with my own family and friends. You discover that you're sort of out of the loop. Your children, if they traveled with you, may miss a whole cycle of cartoons, music, and even sneakers and clothing.

Another factor is the lifestyle. Returning means giving up the posh life associated with assignments abroad. Gone are the coun-try club memberships, maids, drivers, paid housing, and other perks given to those living in other countries. Also be ready to give up the recognition that goes with sort of an ambassadorial status that comes with living in a foreign land. Back in the States, you're just one of many. There is no special treatment.

Returning to work in the United States has its own dilemmas as well. There is less independence. Working overseas, you probably called the shots. Returning to headquarters means bosses, bureaucracy, and all the frustrations that go with it.

If you plan ahead for your return, you will adjust well. But you will need to take an active role in your preparation. Don't wait for your company to initiate it. If you return expecting the company to take care of you, you'll be in for a turbulent period of readjustment.

Be a Singing Waiter

What if you don't connect with a company that will hire you for an overseas assignment but you are still determined to take your career global? Lorne Philips became a singing waiter in a '50s-style burger bar in London's Piccadilly Square and parlayed his exposure in London as a waiter into the investment job of his dreams as an economic analyst in a venture capital firm.

"Working abroad, even as a waiter, exposed me to different ideas and a culture, and that fact impressed my job interviewers," explains Phillips, an economics graduate from Rice University in Houston. "It showed that I wasn't afraid to take risks and that I had an independent spirit," he said in the September 11, 1995, issue of the *Los Angeles Times*.

Where to Get More Information about Taking Your Career Global

The following books and organizations offer information about taking your career global:

1. *Work, Study, Travel Abroad, The Whole World Handbook*, by the Council on International Educational Exchange, St. Martin's Press
2. *International Jobs: Where They Are, How to Get Them*, by Eric Kocher, Addison-Wesley
3. *Work Your Way around The World*, by Susan Griffin, Vacation Work Publishers, Oxford, England
4. *Directory of Overseas Summer Jobs*, by Peterson's Guides, Princeton, NJ
5. *How to Get a Job in Europe*, Surrey Books, Chicago
6. *How to Get a Job in the Pacific Rim*, Surrey Books, Chicago
7. *The Directory of Jobs & Careers Abroad*, by Andre De Vries, distributed in the U.S.A. by Peterson's Guides, Princeton, NJ
8. Council on International Educational Exchange
   205 E. 42nd Street
   New York, NY 10017
9. Japan Information Center
   Consulate General of Japan
   299 Park Ave.
   New York, NY 10017

Source: *International Jobs: Where They Are, How to Get Them*

Where to Get More Information about Taking Your Family Global

The following resource list of books and articles offers additional information about taking your family global:

1. *Bringing up Children Overseas: A Guide for Families*, Sidney Werkman, Basic Books Inc., 1977
2. *Cross-Cultural Reentry: A Book of Readings*, edited by Clyde N. Austin, Ph.D., Abilene Christian University, 1986
3. "The Executive Family: An Overlooked Variable in International Assignments," Michael G. Harvey, *Columbia Journal of Business*, Spring 1985, pp. 84–91.
4. "The Euro-Asian Business Review: The Successful Expatriate Family," Mildred M. McCoy, *The Euro-Asia Centre Inside*, April 1986, Vol. 5, No. 2, pp. 3-10.
5. *The Foreign Service Teenager at Home in the U.S.: A Few Thoughts for Parents Returning with Teenagers*, Kay Branaman Eakin, Foreign Service Institute, US. Department of State, May 1988
6. *Global Parenting*, Available through International Orientation Resources, 500 Skokie Blvd., Suite 600, Northbrook, IL 60062
7. *The ISS Directory of Overseas Schools*, by International Schools Services, Inc., P.O. Box 5910, Princeton, NJ 08543
8. *Notes From a Traveling Childhood: Readings for Internationally Mobile Parents & Children*, edited by Karen Cur-

now McCluskey, Foreign Service Youth Foundation, P.O. Box 39185, Washington, DC 20016

Source: *Personnel Journal*, March 1996.

Growth of Emerging Foreign Markets

According to the U.S. Commerce Department, U.S. companies and global job seekers can expect growth in the following emerging markets into the year 2000 and beyond.

Top Ten Emerging Markets For U.S. Operations

Country	Population	Area in sq. kilometers	Gross Domestic Product (GDP)	Average GDP growth
Mexico	92 million	1, 972,550	$740 billion	0.4%
Brazil	162 million	8,511,965	$785 billion	5%
Argentina	34 million	2,766,890	$185 billion	6%
Poland	38 million	312,680	$180.4 billion	4.1%
Turkey	62 million	780,580	$312.4 billion	7.3%
South Korea	45 million	98,480	$424 billion	6.3%
South Africa	44 million	1,219,912	$171 billion	3.8%
China	1.2 billion	9,636,980	$809 billion	8.3%
Indonesia	200 million	1,919,449	$571 billion	6.5%
India	920 million	3,287,590	$1.7 trillion	3.8%

Source: U.S. Commerce Department

STRATEGY 10

Start Your Own Business

When Tasso entered the executive level of his industry at age twenty-nine, he thought he was on the fast track to success. After four years as director of sales for an elite New York based Italian shoe company, he became disillusioned. He realized he was doing all the work and not really getting sufficient recognition for helping build the company's bottom line. "It was increasingly difficult for me to see my company and managers make all the money," he states.

At age thirty-three, he received an incredible offer at the executive level from another Northeast based Fortune 500 shoe company. Within ten days of employment, he was sure he had made a mistake. He explains, "They were not interested in creativity or what I had to offer. Once I signed the employment contract I was now their property. Their attitude was, 'If we want you to get on a plane and go to South America for three weeks, turn around come back and do it again, you'll do it.' I was not happy with that. What I needed was my independence to be effective at my job. It was very frustrating and restricting. Putting me in a suit and tie every day was like putting a straitjacket on me. I just couldn't deal with it. I left after only a few months of employment."

What Tasso really wanted was his independence. He continues, "When I was not happy, I started to ask myself, What do I do now? I knew I had to start my own company. I listed my top reasons for this, which were to control my own destiny and be independent. I knew enough about my industry and had enough confidence in myself to know I could do a good job. I can't stress too much that my first priority was independence. It was not money. In fact, I spent all the money I saved starting the business."

As with Tasso, a common statistic about entrepreneurs is that the number-one reason the vast majority of them go into business for themselves is for independence. Money is *not* the main motivator. Further, the other reasons entrepreneurs start their own business is for personal expression and creativity, the ability to control their product, so they can make decisions quickly, and for the financial rewards. Owning your own business, you get to do business on your terms. You can do whatever you want and have virtually no supervision. As is with most businesses, there is a downside. You have to be concerned about the money every day, collections, creditors, the people side of the business, hiring, firing, decision making at high levels, management, and supervision.

As the future world of work evolves, increasingly there will be more opportunities to become self-employed and achieve personal independence. With the advent of the personal computer, this technology alone has made it possible now more than any time before to start and own your own business. Across the nation, as a great number of executives fall victim to downsizing, starting a business may very well be the next step for many. As soon as the paychecks stop coming in and they become disillusioned with corporate life, a new dream of being independent will emerge.

Are You Psychologically Suited to Start Your Own Business?

The idea of starting your own business may be a good idea, but success is hardly guaranteed. It takes more than desire to launch and build your own business. In fact, it is a long and arduous task. The SBA (Small Business Administration) says the average business takes ten months to two years before it turns a profit. In the meantime there are a lot of obstacles, challenges, and setbacks. Growing the business requires a wide range of responsibilities such as business accounting, sales, operations, marketing, management, and even cleaning. In the corporate world you were responsible for only one part of the whole. In your own business, however, you play the part of all the roles combined each and every day.

For instance, a computer consultant left a good job at IBM to start her own training company. For four months her diet consisted of peanut butter sandwiches, beans, and rice. She did not dine out for a year just so she could cover her business expenses. But in her case, the sacrifice was within her psychological

makeup. She was dedicated to succeeding. She could delay gratification. As a result, it took her only a year before she turned a
profit.

The Entrepreneur Profile Test

Before your embark on your own business, consider whether you
have the psychological profile necessary to be an entrepreneur.
Take a look at the following questions and answer each one truth-
fully. At the end of each question rate your response on a scale
from one to ten. One represents *never* and ten *always*.

The Test

1. I have managed significant and important projects without
   supervision. _____
2. I like to initiate projects and have excellent follow-
   through. _____
3. When it comes to being in charge, I enjoy the challenge
   and the role. _____
4. I have no problem hiring and firing others when its necessary. _____
5. Delegating work is how I get most of my projects
   done. _____
6. I criticize others' work when necessary and get what I need
   from them. _____
7. I don't mind selling, negotiating, or compromising when I
   have to. _____

8. I am a highly energetic and enthusiastic individual. _____

9. I am able to delay gratification, such as putting off purchasing luxuries in order to achieve my goals in life. _____

10. I consider myself to be an excellent time manager and my work area to be neat, clean, and organized. _____

Your Score

Go ahead and add up your total score. If you have a composite score of fifty or less, consider the fact that it is highly improbable that you have the unique abilities to be a successful small business owner. In fact, whether you embark on your own venture or remain in the corporate environment, your aversion to risk will hold you back. If you scored in the sixties, seventies, eighties, or above, you are in those same increments more likely to take chances and succeed. In fact, if you scored in the nineties, you are ready to embark on your own business. If you choose to remain in the corporate arena, it may also mean that you will make a very successful "intrepreneur." The decision is up to you.

What if you were not psychologically suited to being on your own? All is not lost to fulfill your desire for independence. Begin now to develop yourself right where you're at. Begin to take on projects at the company where you are currently employed. Crave and desire projects and let your voice be known to corporate leadership. They will not normally come to you. You must begin today to assert yourself and go to them with your creativity and ideas for change. Get ready for rejection, too. Learn how to not take it personally and remain persistent. Don't ask for more money and benefits, either. Remember you are doing this to build your own skills. Begin now to grow and challenge yourself daily. Be committed to personal growth whether it is inside or outside the corporate world.

Helpful Statistics

Before trading in corporate life for owning your own business, you should know what kind of hours you will work and some other facts about small business (ten employees or less) ownership.

- Being self-employed is a common fantasy among workers. When polled about their dream job, women and men put owning their own business within their top five responses. The idea of ownership taps into the imagination of freedom from bosses, policies, procedures, and restricted personal time off.
- As more women have bumped up against the glass ceiling, the invisible barrier beyond which women cannot advance in the corporate world, many will increasingly turn to owning their own businesses. Nearly one-third of all entrepreneurs surveyed by the Internal Revenue Service in 1987 were female; going into the twenty-first century, it is estimated women will own half of all businesses.
- Another study done by the SBA found that one out of four businesses dissolves within the first two years of operations. It has been discovered that one of the most prevalent reasons for business failures was insufficient capital.

- Small business owners work an average of 52.5 hours per week. Other Americans work an average of 43.5 hours.
- Entrepreneurs become self-employed at an average age of 28.7 years.
- Currently, males dominate small business ownership three to one.
- Sixty-three percent say independence or the opportunity to be their own boss is the main reason for self-employment.

Sources: SBA, IRS, and National Association for the Self-Employed

Up All Night

David frequently pulls all-nighters in Colorado Springs, Colorado, where he owns David Swaney and Associates. Sure, life as an entrepreneur is tough, but would he give it all up to work again for someone else? Would he give up his independence? Would he even trade the joys of being self-employed for a night of restful sleep? "Never," he states in an article, "Sounding Off," that he wrote for the January 1966 issue of *Entrepreneur* Magazine. He continues:

The alarm clock says 3:20 a.m. In four hours, I'm supposed to make a major presentation to a new client, and here I am wide awake. My head has been spinning with anxiety, mild vertigo and wild dreams since I laid it on the pillow three hours ago. If I don't get some sleep, I'm going to feel like day-old Cream of Wheat when I crawl out of bed at six. How will I ever be able to sell the capabilities of my small editorial services company? I'll barely be able to utter my own name.

If I take one of my killer-but-always-puts-me-right-to-sleep pills now, I won't fully wake up until two hours after the meeting is over. With this big appointment coming up, I should never have tried the New Age cure for insomnia, clove tea, suggested by the woman at the herb store. I should have realized that since cloves make my gums numb to a toothache, why wouldn't clove tea have the same effect on my brain?

Like many restless entrepreneurs, my search for a remedy to help me sleep has become something akin to a quest for the Holy Grail. Clove tea was merely the latest dead end in my hunt. The only thing I've discovered for sure is that there is a zillion cures for insomnia . . . and most of them don't work.

Indeed, there are almost as many ways to treat insomnia as there are business owners who can't get a decent night's rest. I've tried everything—prayer, sedatives, self-help, Nyquil, exercise, chamomile tea, Tylenol PM, late-night television, even, in a last, desperate attempt, reading software documentation.

The problem is stress; that much I know. Running a frantically busy, deadline-obsessive business every day gets my adrenaline pumping madly. The only cure that consistently works is my killer-but-always-puts-me-right-to-sleep Halcion pill. I hate to use it, but if there's one thing I hate more, it's tossing and turning all night. At times, I've taken Halcion for two and three weeks straight.

Actually, I know there's a better cure, one that would

let me enjoy night after night of safe and restful sleep: I could get a stress-free job. But I *love* running my own business. There's nothing like the freedom of working for yourself, that feeling of shaping your own destiny, the eternal hope that a rich mother lode might make itself known with the next ring of the phone. A no-stress job would be a fate worse than death.

So I lie there hallucinating in my clove-induced spell. I spend 10 minutes wondering what might happen if I combine the effects of the clove tea and Halcion. They'd probably have to wheel me into the meeting on a dolly. I think about my life—which sleeplessness aside, has never been happier.

Top Ten Strategies for Starting Your Own Business

After reading Dave's story and this chapter thus far, if you are still convinced you are ready to start your own business, here are my top ten strategies for doing it. The recommendations are based on over sixteen ventures I have initiated over the years as well as years of networking and discussing small business ventures with other entrepreneurs.

1. *Keep start-up money to a minimum.* Don't go into debt or risk the family savings. It's not worth it for a new business venture that statistically has a 20 to 30 percent chance of succeeding. Devise a business and plan that can be started with existing ideas, your inherent talent, ingenuity, and very little cash.

2. *Learn to sell yourself.* As a small business owner, people are buying you, not your product. Once you are confident you know how to sell yourself, having large sums of start-up money is not important. You will be landing accounts within your first thirty days of operations. Cash flow will begin within sixty days, and that will help to begin to fuel your company's growth.

3. *Don't be selfish with your new company and services.* A new venture is not always the best time to be price gouging your initial clients. In fact, in my opinion, it is the exact opposite. In many cases, I've initially had to give my services away to let clients begin to try me just to see what I could do. Even if they did not eventually go to contract, they served as excellent references for the next paying customer. Sometimes you have to give a little to get a lot.

4. *Initiate a product or service that you can launch right out of your own home.* I once started a consulting company in the corner of my bedroom with only a desk, chair, and small computer. Within five years the business grew to over a half million in revenues, was located in its own office building, and twelve employees worked there. Start with a small, manageable idea and grow.

5. *Begin the business from day one on computer-based technology.* Typewriters and other manual methods are no longer competitive in the current marketplace. From correspondence, accounting, marketing, lead generation, and sales, *you just won't be able to compete.* Start your company from day one on a computer.

6. *Work long hours.* Keep administrative tasks such as accounting and correspondence for the evening hours. That should *never* be done during the hours of nine to five. Prime business

hours have only one purpose for a successful small business owner and that is to network, present to, talk to, telephone, and sell new clients face-to-face. After a complete day of seeing clients, then it is time to come home and begin nonrevenue-generating activities such as correspondence and administration. Welcome to the "fun" of being an entrepreneur!

7. *Love your customers.* Always speak politely to them no matter how much they may anger you at times. Remember, the customer is not only king and queen, but dictator. Nobody knows this more than a small business owner. Be committed to customer satisfaction. My belief has always been to contract for one set of services but in the end to always *exceed* the customer's expectations. Go beyond your contract. Routinely deliver more than what your customers expect. That is the best form of advertisement there is for a small business owner.

8. *If at first you don't succeed, try, try again.* Never, never give up. Success is usually right on the other side of failure. If you are failing, then you are on the right track. Just increase your failures and if you try long enough, with some intelligent choices along the way, you will succeed.

9. *Go into business for yourself.* Avoid start-up situations where you invite into the company working and capital partners. Partners are like marriages. Are you ready for that commitment? Especially when in the partnership of marriage alone, statistically one in two ends up in divorce. If you're going to start a business, generally speaking, you are better off on your own. However, only you can make that decision.

10. *Take time to relax.* I have forced myself many times to take a Satuday or Sunday off despite a backlog of enormous amounts of administration and correspondence. The day you lose will be

restored back to you many times with increased productivity in the coming week. Also, your family and clients will thank you for it as well, as you will appear calmer and more agreeable in your dealings with others. Take time for some exercise, a family outing, or even a movie that will help you escape your mental focus on the business. You will be a much more effective business owner as a result of it.

In Summary

To declare your own independence, you need a sense of adventure, lots of guts, and an incredible belief in yourself. A person running his or her own business should learn more about the technical and financial aspects, especially if the individual is more experienced and focused on the creative side of the business. Computer knowledge is a must. Be prepared to work more than forty hours a week. Be ready to accept short-term pain for long-term gain.

Remember, there is an alternative to working for another big company. It just might be owning your own business. It just might be for you.

BIBLIOGRAPHY

Abisheganaden, Felix. "Some Ideas for Personal and Career Development," *New Straits Times*, June 6, 1995, sec. Personal Development.

American Society for Training and Development. September 1992, Vol. 46; No. 9; p. 77.

Cooney, Roman. "No Pay, No Perks, No Promotions, but Volunteer Work Brings Results," *Calgary Herald*, November 16, 1994, Final Edition, sec. Commentary.

Davis, Tim, "Using Psychotherapy to Deal with Mental Health Problems in Organizations," *Business Horizons*, March 1991, Vol. 34; No. 2; p. 56.

De Vries, Andre. *The Directory of Jobs and Careers Abroad*. Surrey, England: The Gresham Press, 1993.

Federal Information Systems Corporation. "Prepared Statement of Jef-

Bibliography

frey H. Joseph, RE: Educational Technology in the 21st Century," *Federal News Service*, October 12, 1995.

Flynn, Gillian. "Telecommuters Report Higher Productivity—and Better Home Lives," *Personnel Journal*, November 1995, p. 23.

Foord-Kirk, Janis. "Create a Job by Selling What's in Your Head," *The Toronto Star*, July 25, 1991, Saturday Edition, sec. C, Feature.

Grappo, Gary Joseph. *Get The Job You Want In Thirty Days*. New York: Berkley, 2nd edition, 1997.

———. *The Top 10 Fears of Job Seekers*. New York: Berkley, 1996.

Greengard, Samuel. "All the Comforts of Home," *Personnel Journal*, July 1995, p. 104.

Handy, Charles. *The Age of Paradox*. Boston, MA: Harvard Business School Press, 1994.

———. *The Age of Unreason*. Boston, MA: Harvard Business School Press, 1990.

Hardin, Patricia. "Job Security Continues to Plummet," *Personnel Journal*, September 1995, p. 19.

Hodges, Jill. "International Work Assignments Challenge Employees, Families," *Star Tribune*, November 5, 1995, Metro Edition, sec. D, Marketplace.

Howard, Lucy. "Want to Start Your Own Business?" *Newsweek*, November 26, 1990, sec. Periscope; p. 8.

Information Access Company, A Thomson Corporation. "Survey of Current Business," *U.S. Department Of Commerce*, July 1995, Vol. 75; No. 7; p. 44.

Bibliography

Information Access Company, A Thomson Corporation. "On The Trail Of Wily Homos Jobus Hoppus," *RV Business*, February 1996, Vol. 46; No. 11; p. 28.

Kitchen, Patricia. "Get Ready for a New Start," *Newsday*, April 17, 1994, All Editions, sec. Career Forum.

Kleiman, Carol. *The 100 Best Jobs for the 1990s and Beyond.* New York: Berkley, 1994.

————. "Youth Give New Meaning to Upward Mobility," *Chicago Tribune*, June 29, 1994, North Sports Final Edition, sec. C, Your Money.

Laabs, Jennifer J. "HR Pioneers Explore the Road Less Traveled," *Personnel Journal*, February 1996, p. 70.

La Ganga, Maria L. "International Careers: A World of Opportunity: Top Ten Emerging Markets for U.S. Operations," *Los Angeles Times*, September 11, 1995, Home Edition, sec. D, Business.

Lawlor, Judy. "Selling Yourself Key to Job Hunt," *USA Today*, May 13, 1991, Final Edition, sec. B, Money.

Lazzareschi, Carla. "International Careers: A World of Opportunity: Word Abroad Can Boost Prospects at Home," *Los Angeles Times*, September 11, 1995, Home Edition, sec. D, Business.

Luciano, Lani. "Five Smart Ways to Get Ahead Today," *Money*, March 1995, p. 118.

McDermott, Lynda. "Marketing Yourself as 'Me, Inc.'," *Training and Development*, September 1992, Vol. 46; No. 9; p. 77.

McGarvey, Robert. "Just Do It," *Entrepreneur*, January 1996.

Bibliography

Moon, Mimi. "Why Not Start Your Own Business?" *Sacramento Bee*, August 19, 1994, Metro Final Edition, sec. Scene.

Moss, Tim. "U.S. Secretary of Labor Robert Reich on the Future of Work," *Details*, January 1996, p. 42.

Peters, Tom. *Liberation Management*. New York: Fawcett Columbine, 1992.

———. *The Tom Peters Seminar*. New York: Vintage Books, 1994.

Phinney, Susan. "Tight Market Requires Sharp Job-Hunting Skills," *The Orlando Sentinel*, January 27, 1994, sec. E, Style.

PR Newswire Association, Inc. "Careers 2000 Online Networking Can Mean The Job Finds You," *PR Newswire*, June 13, 1995.

Quinn, Matthew C. "A Hot Spot for Work; Atlanta Job Growth to Lead U.S. through 2000," *The Atlanta Constitution*, November 15, 1995, All Editions, sec. Business.

Read, Roland. "Want To Start Your Own Business?" *Public Relations Journal*, October 1993, p. 3.

Rose. "Truer to Life High School," *The Orlando Sentinel*, May 15, 1995, Metro Edition, sec. A, Editorial.

S. G., "What's All This Talk about Gophers?" *Personnel Journal*, July 1995, p. 66.

Sander, Marcus I. "Fourteen Steps on a New Career Path," *HRMagazine*, March 1993, Vol. 38; No. 3; p. 55.

Satterfield, Mark. "Give Yourself the Stress Test: Strategy, Exercise Helps Take the Tension out of Your Job Hunt," *The Atlanta Constitution*, September 29, 1991, All Editions, sec. R; Job Guide.

Bibliography

Scheele, Adele. "Your Fantasy Career: Should You Go For It?" *Working Woman*, January, 1991, Vol. 16; No. 1; p. 34.

Scott, Niki. "Don't Let Others Block Career Advancement," *The Courier-Journal*, January 16, 1991, Metro Edition, sec. C, Features.

Silver, A. David. *Quantum Companies*. Princeton, NJ: Peterson's/Pacesetter Books, 1995.

Stevens, Mark. "It Takes More Than Desire to Start Your Own Business," *Star Tribune*, November 22, 1993, Metro Edition, sec. Marketplace; Small business.

Swaney, David. "Sounding Off," *Entrepreneur*, January, 1996, p. 368.

Toffler, Alvin. *Future Shock*. New York: Bantam Books, 1990.

———. *Power Shift*. New York: Bantam Books, 1990.

Walberg, Marvin. "Positive Attitude Creates a Winning Record in Football and in Job Search," *Rocky Mountain News*, March 6, 1994, sec. F, Careers.

Correspond with the
Author Directly on
the Internet

Mr. Grappo appreciates hearing from readers of his books and participants in his seminars. Write when you have an experience to share. Success stories based on the use of his concepts are always welcome. Also, to order quantities of his books or to reach the author for a speaking engagement, send E-mail to: gjgjoseph@aol.com.